JENNIFER STRICKLAND

Endorsements

For every girl who is ready to put aside the mask of pretense. For every girl who longs for authenticity. For every girl who desires to be set free. You will find what you are looking for in the pages of this powerful study! This is a treasure chest full of truth, that when applied, will absolutely change your life!

CHRISTINA DIMARI
AUTHOR, *OCEAN STAR* & *YOU'RE DESIGNED TO SHINE*

Jen has poured out her heart to Him and He has conveyed His grace for you through these very pages. I dare you to not just treat this as "yet-another-small-group-blah-blah-study-guide" BUT to genuinely and authentically step into it with an open mind and willing heart, with the warning: if you do, your life will NEVER be the same again. I know, because mine isn't. Thank you, Jen, for declaring the truth as beauty in His sight.

BRONWEN HEALY
SPEAKER/AUTHOR/FOUNDER, *HOPE FOUNDATION, AUSTRALIA*

As a Christian Counselor in private practice, God has given me many teens and young adults to work with who suffer with strongholds such as self-injury, eating disorders, mood disorders, anxiety disorders, and personality disorders. As I peel away the layers of their pain with them, I find that at the core, in most cases, is a lack of identity in Christ. The *Girl Perfect Study Guide* will be a tremendous asset and tool that God can use to bring healing to their hurt and His identity to their confused and searching souls.

LAUREL SLADE, M.S.
BOARD CERTIFIED CHRISTIAN COUNSELOR

Jennifer Strickland is one of my favorite communicators. *The Girl Perfect Study Guide* is filled with life-changing content and practical ideas. Jennifer understands the heart and soul of women. Don't miss this transforming experience for your life.

JIM BURNS, PH.D.
PRESIDENT, *HOMEWORD*
AUTHOR, *CREATING AN INTIMATE MARRIAGE AND CONFIDENT PARENTING*

The *Girl Perfect Study Guide* shatters the lies girls and women believe and points to the ultimate truth which really does set us free. I am confident that this study will help thousands discover a beauty, purpose, and worth that truly lasts. Thank you Jen for exposing the "perfect lie" and inviting girls to experience God's "perfect love."

ALLIE MARIE SMITH
FOUNDER & AUTHOR, *WONDERFULLY MADE*

What a high calling it is to heal from past lies and live in power and purity provided by God. Jennifer Strickland's *Girl Perfect Study Guide* is a life-changing message that is written with passion and underlined with the Word of God. I can't wait to give to our granddaughters!

JUDY W. HALLIDAY
CO-FOUNDER, *THIN WITHIN MINISTRIES*

The *Girl Perfect Study Guide* is the compelling personal journey of Jennifer Strickland intricately woven with persuasive biblical passages that propel the reader toward concrete solutions. This study guide takes you deeper into your understanding of the divine grace of Jesus Christ because of God's never ending love.

DEVI TITUS
PRESIDENT, *OF GLOBAL PASTORS WIVES NETWORK*
SPEAKER/AUTHOR/FOUNDER, *MENTORING MANSION & HOME EXPERIENCE*

Do you hate to see a grown man cry? Then don't let him read Jennifer Strickland's *Girl Perfect Study Guide*. That is precisely what I did when I read Jennifer's manuscript. This isn't your ordinary boring, pedantic workbook; it's alive in the Spirit and capable of bringing life to all who read it. So go ahead and cry with me. It's cathartic. Just don't tell your husband that you saw him crying.

LARRY TITUS
PRESIDENT, *KINGDOM GLOBAL MINISTRIES*
AUTHOR, *THE TELEIOS MAN, YOUR ULTIMATE IDENTITY*

The *P* word may be the heaviest burden women bear. All the misguided things that we do to gain it, keep us away from what we need most...the unconditional love of God the Father. Jennifer tells us what, why, and how in this study guide, a map toward the wholeness we were created for.

NANCY ORTBERG
AUTHOR AND FORMER TEACHING PASTOR,
WILLOW CREEK COMMUNITY CHURCH

Girl Perfect Study Guide – A Journey Through the Longings of our Hearts
by Jennifer Strickland

Published by FaithHappenings Publishers
7500 E. Arapahoe Rd., Suite 285
Centennial, CO 80112
303.471.6675
admin@wordserveliterary.com

This book or parts thereof may not be reproduced in any form, stored in a retrieval system, or transmitted in any form by any means—electronic, mechanical, photocopy, recording, or otherwise—without prior written permission of the publisher, except as provided by United States of America copyright law.

Unless otherwise noted, Scripture quotations are from The Holy Bible: NEW INTERNATIONAL VERSION ®. Copyright © 1973, 1978, 1984 by Biblica, Inc. All rights reserved worldwide. Used by permission.

Scripture quotations noted KJV are from The Holy Bible: King James Version. Cambridge, 1769. Used by permission. All rights reserved.

Scripture quotations noted GNT are from the Good News Translation-Second Edition. Copyright © 1992 by American Bible Society. Used by permission.

Scripture quotations noted The Message are from the The Message. Copyright © 1993, 1994, 1996, 2000, 2001, 2002. Used by permission of NavPress Publishing Group.

Scripture quotations noted NAS are from the New American Standard Bible ®. Copyright © 1960, 1962, 1963, 1968, 1971, 1972, 1973, 1975, 1977, 1995 by the Lockman Foundation. Used by permission.

Scripture quotations noted NLT are from the Holy Bible, New Living Translation. Copyright © 1996 and 2004. Used by permission of Tyndale House Publishers, Wheaton, Illinois 60189. All rights reserved.

Highlighted Reading selections in this book are from Girl Perfect, published by FaithHappenings Publishers, a division of WordServe Literary, © 2023 by Jennifer Strickland. All rights reserved.

ISBN 13: 9781941555590

Reprint Edition published in 2023
First published by Higher Life books, 2008

Printed in the United States of America

For Our Daughter,

We will tell the next generation the praiseworthy deeds of the LORD, his power, and the wonders he has done.

Psalm 78:4b

Acknowledgments

The following people have been my partners in this work. They have given of themselves to bring this baby to birth, and I pray joy fills their hearts for its new life.

To my Beloved Husband ...
Shane: Greatest thanks go to you. You have held my hand through many seasons of healing. Thank you for your sacrifice, your faith in me, and for continuing to unabashedly lead our family in the dreams God has for us. I love you.

To the Girls ...
Mom: Here we go again! I'm taking off the masks, getting real, and lives are changing! Thank you for believing in and supporting my dreams—time and time again.
Linda Strickland: my mother-in-love: I couldn't have done it without you. Thank you for making this dream possible. As you quietly guide me in the background, you are impacting a generation who needs to learn from you. By your life, you have taught us the real meaning of beauty.
Olivia: Thank you for your encouragement, sacrifice, and faith in your Mama. I am so proud to call you Daughter.
Jan Alexander and Caris Leidner: You are my left hand and my right. My deepest gratitude for your hard work behind the scenes, tireless research, and most of all, your faith in this ministry and example of what it is to pursue with passion the mission of instilling value in women and girls.
Debbie Eaton: God has used you to bring this to his daughters. I am awed by your faith.
Devi Titus: My mama bird, who knew she was assigned to me the moment she met me. Thank you for putting me under your wing.
Megan Carter, Kristen Smith, and the prayer team: We did it together!
All the women and girls who have reached out to me: You were at the center of my heart as I wrote.

To the Boys ...
Greg Johnson: You put it all together so I could write. Thank you so much for believing!
Steve Arterburn and Jim Burns: When I walked into your offices years ago, you watered the seed planted in me, and you continue to water it.
Larry Titus: You made me believe that others could be changed through the journey. Thank you.

Dad, Papa, and Greg: You have been generous, gracious, and faithful. I am so grateful for your consistent love and support in my life.
Zach and Sam: You have shown me the beauty of what it is to come to Jesus with the faith of a little child. Thank you and I love you all.

To Karen Amaral, David Welday, Alice Bass, Marsha McCoy, Deborah Poulalion, Rebecca A. Russo, and the team at Higher Life and Strang: Hallelujah! Well done! Thank you for not treating me as plastic, for seeing my heart, and sending it to press. You are reaching many.

Table of Contents

Endorsements 3
Acknowledgments 9
Introduction 13
Some Notes to Begin Your Journey 19

Lesson 1 — The Little Girl Inside of You 23
Lesson 2 — The Longing to Be Affirmed 27
Lesson 3 — Sex 35
Lesson 4 — Shame 45
Lesson 5 — Made New 53
Lesson 6 — Jealousy and Comparisons 61
Lesson 7 — The Domino Effect 69
Lesson 8 — Eyes of Grace 77
Lesson 9 — Unveiled 85
Lesson 10 — Taking Off The Masks 93
Lesson 11 — The Lord and The Body 105
Lesson 12 — The Longing and The Hunger 113
Lesson 13 — Perfection and The Body 121
Lesson 14 — Looking Good 131
Lesson 15 — Beautiful and Glorious 141
Lesson 16 — Money, Money, Money 151
Lesson 17 — Treasures in Heaven 159
Lesson 18 — The Threefold Dream Part 1: The Spirit 165
Lesson 19 — The Threefold Dream Part 2: The Crown 177
Lesson 20 — The Threefold Dream Part 3: The Plan 187
Lesson 21 — Captivity and Exile 201
Lesson 22 — Going Into Hiding: False Methods of Escape 211
Lesson 23 — The Wide Path or The Narrow? 223
Lesson 24 — A Little Girl Again 235
Lesson 25 — The Perfect Path 243
Lesson 26 — Our Food 255
Lesson 27 — Healing Waters 263
Lesson 28 — Freedom to be the Girl God Made 271
Lesson 29 — Free Indeed 277
Lesson 30 — My Canaan 283

A Worksheet: What Is Perfect? 287
The Lies, The Longings, and The Truths That Set Us Free 289
Notes 291

Introduction

Dear Girlfriends,

It took me years to gather the courage to write *Girl Perfect: Confessions of a Former Runway Model* because it was a labor of love borne from significant pain. Like any labor, it hurt. It was difficult to return to the darkest pits of my life and write openly about the turmoil I experienced there. At the same time, it was a sweet joy to recall in detail the many miracles that ushered me into a life of faith. The ultimate challenge I faced in writing the book was finally letting go of the desire to get it perfect—to physically, mentally, and emotionally release it from my grip and let it sail into the world to find its own destinations.

In labor, the birth hurts the most, and then we forget about the pain as we marvel at the new life that came from us. In the same way, the anguish of birthing the book has brought forth a living instrument of truth and hope that was breathed by the Spirit of God to a hurting generation. Every day I wrote, I began on my knees, praying that God would speak to the heart of every woman and girl through the story. Today there are no bounds to the joy I possess from knowing that by being honest in the book, I have seen others set free to be honest as well.

Nevertheless, I know the book is not enough. That is where the *Girl Perfect Study Guide* comes in. I have heard from many hurting souls around the world who are struggling with eating disorders, self-harm, depression, anxiety, addiction, abuse, rejection, betrayal, loss, and broken hearts that come in an endless kaleidoscope of patterns. They read my book and wrote me gut-wrenchingly honest letters, describing often in detail the tremendous pain they have suffered. Many have inspired me by telling how they too have been set free, healed, and made whole by the One who made them. From their stories, I realized that a deeper journey is both sought after and called for. So as hard as it has been for me to go back again to those places of despair, I have done it in this guide in firm belief that if we dive deeper into the longings of our hearts, we will find that which will fill them, and we will come up from the swim cleansed and healed.

It is my hope that this study guide is the springboard that launches you into a deeper journey for yourself. I never wrote the book to be about me. It has always been about you—no matter your age or life story. This book is about the journey we all have in search of freedom from the chains that bind us from reaching our full potential—fulfilled and at peace with who we are. This study guide is only that—a guide—to usher you along this journey to freedom and to help you guide others. For that is the calling of every woman on earth: to become all that God designed her to be, and to inspire others to do the same.

The Question of Age

Because I have shared my story with women and girls from nine to ninety-nine, I know that it resonates with all ages (and men too, might I add!). But because I feel personally responsible to speak to the generation of girls coming up behind me, I wrote the book with young women in mind. The plague of lies about our real beauty and value as women has become more "in-your-face" for this generation – thanks to social media – however the question of women's worth is a timeless one. So if you are in your thirties or older, this book and study are still for you. Women of all generations have been wounded and crippled, and the older we are, the more healing we need.

The other picture I imagined while writing is of the little girl—maybe eight years old or so—who loses her innocence over time and becomes jaded and hurt by the cruelty of life on earth. This girl is within us all. We all have an eight-year-old little girl living inside of us who longs for love, peace, and freedom. We all have our stories about how those longings have been met or unmet. On the inside, we are each the same.

Yet there is no question that the world of girls losing themselves in screens has frustrated older, wiser women. Many of our mothers and grandmothers feel utterly disconnected to the younger girl perfects who are snapping, scrolling, posting, liking... or piercing, starving, and even outright rejecting their bodies in search of fulfillment. The younger ones are grasping for individuality and authenticity, using their voices in all kinds of ways – from how they dress, to the pictures they post, to the videos they create – often standing as polar opposites to their more reserved mothers and grandmothers. But it is God's design that the older women stand arm-in-arm with the younger. It is our assignment to get inside of their world and help them navigate it.

So to the older women (that includes me), I say, read the book and do the study for you. But, do it also for your daughter and granddaughter and great-granddaughter, to better understand and empathize with the little girl inside of her, who lives in a world obsessed with image and who is looking for truth and wanting to see it *in you*.

To the younger woman, I say, thank you for being brave. You are the future, and the more you know about your real beauty, value, and purpose, the more powerful you will be. I'm proud of you for getting real, and *I'm for you*. I encourage you to be aware of the lies this study exposes – for you and for your friends – and memorize the truths. If you do, you will change the destination of your life, and the lives you touch.

The Pep Talk

In the book of Joshua, God gave Joshua a serious pep talk before Joshua went out to guide the people into the land across the Jordan. He said, "As I was with Moses, so I will be with you; I will never leave you nor forsake you" (1:5). God continued to tell Joshua repetitively to be "strong and courageous," "to be strong and very courageous." He instructed Joshua to carefully obey all of the Law, to meditate on God's Word day and night, and to follow God's leadership through the tumultuous waters of the Jordan and the battles over the fruitful land of Canaan that lay beyond it. God promised Joshua that if Joshua followed these instructions, he would be prosperous and successful, and his Lord would be with him wherever he went (Josh. 1:6–9).

One of the most fascinating things to me in the book of Joshua is what the Israelite leaders said to the people right before they crossed the Jordan River. Their leaders explained why the people had to be very careful to follow their directions, saying, "Then you will know which way to go, *since you have never been this way before*" (Josh. 3:4a, emphasis added). Please don't assume you've gone this way before and you don't need to follow anyone's lead. Don't give up and go your own way in the middle of the study because it's too hard. Be tough, be strong, be courageous, and follow a free woman to freedom, if you know what I mean. It is the Lord, I assure you, who leads the way.

Our ability to impact a generation with hope begins with breaking free from our own pasts and pain, with laying it all out so God can restore us to wholeness. Only then can we turn and shine a light for others enslaved by the world's lies. In this guide, we will identify those lies and replace them with truth. We will ask questions so your heart may supply the answers. We will go through uncharted waters within us, knowing that we do not go alone. If we stick with it, I believe with all my heart we will come up from the seas of our hearts more whole, free, and wise than we were when we ventured in.

There is no question that going through this guide will bring you deeper than solely reading *Girl Perfect* on its own. You must be strong and courageous to do it because it will be more challenging than just reading the book and walking away. But it will also be incredibly more rewarding.

So be brave, open, real, strong, deliberate, and obedient to the One who is calling you to go a way you have not gone before. This is a journey in which we trust the Lord to lead us when we can't see the finished end. Remember, he led his people through the Jordan to bring them to a place he could see all along—the promised land.

The fullest of cups are the ones who have known what it is to be empty, cast aside, and lifeless; the brightest of lights are those who were once snuffed out and shrouded in darkness; and the strongest of women are those who have survived quicksand and crawled, muddy and desperate, to the Rock upon which they immovably stand.

Once again, I humbly set before you these words, ask the Lord to bless and multiply them, and present to you my heart—that you too may be filled, healed, and freed—and your daughter, and her daughter, and her daughter's daughters...

With love,

Jen

SOME NOTES TO BEGIN YOUR JOURNEY

For this newly revised edition, I have changed very little from the original version. The truths about beauty, body image, success, and fulfillment have not changed at all; but what has changed is the state of girls' hearts. More teen girls are struggling than ever. Isolation, phones, and social media have all led to increased depression and anxiety, and hook-up culture has done us no favors. Whatever age you are, we just need to realize the next generation needs us to be real about what they are facing, and the more we create an environment of openness, the better.

There is no judgment over the words you write in this study; it is a private conversation between you and God alone. He only wants your heart; he's not interested in you creating an image of perfection. Just do you, and do it with all your heart, and he will meet you in these pages.

I use the New International Version Bible translation in this study. You can use any translation you want, but for the fill-in-the-blanks, it may be easier to use the NIV.

Whether you are using this guide in a mentoring group, counseling session, Bible study group, or on your own, I highly suggest you take the time to fill in the blanks and record your answers. It will inspire you to go back and see the journey you have taken. Writing down how you feel now and rereading it later can be a profound testament to growth and how far you've come.

There are several ways you can do this study, depending on your leader's intuition as to what is best for the group or on your personality if you are doing it individually (which I believe is just as beneficial, by the way). You can put your feet up as most girls and women do and read the book *Girl Perfect* in its entirety. Then you can go back with the *Girl Perfect Study Guide* in hand as a way to go deeper. Or you can read the book a chapter at a time, doing the study guide as you go. Another option still is to read two or three chapters and then stop, do the study on those chapters, and continue on. This is your journey, so far be it from me to tell you how to do it.

The suggested readings from *Girl Perfect* throughout the study guide are guideposts that will help refresh your memory as to the subjects raised in the chapter and be a good jumping off point to begin your group discussion and/or personal reflection time as you answer the questions. You are free to choose other sections to read aloud in your group or to reread to yourself.

As you read the book, I encourage you to do so with a highlighter, pen, or even a stack of sticky notes. Write all over it if you want to! Going back through it and seeing what stood out to you can be very beneficial. Bring the book and the study guide with you to your group meetings. You may want to share some of the things that you highlighted.

The *Girl Perfect Study Guide* is divided into 30 lessons based on the 10 chapters of the book. It is designed to do whatever pace works best for you. The important thing is to finish the material for those lessons by the time the group meets. Each chapter of the book has a "Lie," a "Longing," and a "Truth." The first part of the chapter uncovers the lie the world tells us and defines the longing of our hearts that the lie exploits; then the final section reveals the truth that sets us free to get that longing filled in the way God intended. Be sure you get to the last part because you will want to claim the truth!

Please remember that this study guide is in no way exhaustive on the subjects it raises. It goes as deep as we can in this context. But if you suffer from certain issues raised in the study, I have provided suggestions for further reading and references at www.girlperfectbook.com to help you get help in those specific areas. I am not a counselor. I am simply a girl who saw a lot of darkness on earth, clawed her way into a life of light, and now looks to heaven for her guidance. My intention is only to share my experience and hold out my hand to guide you in yours.

Finally, get real. Don't do this if you are going to play the fake game. It will be a waste of everyone's time. If you are going to do this study, do it with an honest, open heart. Be real about where you are, where you've been, and where you hope to be. Don't pretend! In your personal study, nothing will produce more powerful change in you than being open, honest, and real. Your answers written in the guide aren't being judged by anyone, so you might as well lay your heart right open before God and yourself. (He can see through the mask anyway!)

And when you are sharing in the group, I encourage you to ditch the masquerade that divides us and get real with each other. There may be things you don't feel comfortable sharing, and that is okay. But do not pretend to have it all together when you don't. Honesty and realness produce authentic change and develop lasting inner beauty. As I say in the book, "Real is beautiful."

Got it? Great.

Let's Begin!

Girl Perfect Readings

Introduction

Chapter 1—The Perfect Affirmation:
Guys and Sexuality

Lessons

1: The Little Girl Inside of You

2: The Longing to be Affirmed

3: Sex

4: Shame

5: Made New

Lesson 1
The Little Girl Inside of You

Read or reread *Girl Perfect*, the Introduction.

Verse of the Day: "Then [Jesus] said to them, 'Whoever welcomes this little child in my name welcomes me...'" Luke 9:48a

Use the space below to remember that little girl inside of you—that part of you that was once completely innocent. Even if your innocence was robbed at an early age, we all have a little girl within. For you, what was she like? What did she look like? How old is she? If you'd like, name her. Was she free? Was she smart? Talented? What did she like to do? How did she express herself? Take the time before we launch into the longings of your little-girl heart to define that little girl within you. Using the space below, write about her. I encourage you to cut out a picture of yourself as a child and paste it in the left-hand column—or you can draw one – whatever medium helps you recall who you were at your most childlike state.

Masks

> **Highlighted Reading:** "But in order to make it as a model, I had to learn to wear the masks that hid my true self. And I did. I wore them so well even my own parents could not always see through them" (p. 8).

Even if you consider yourself a free person, you have had to wear a mask of pretense at one time or another in your life. For some of us, projecting an image that isn't true becomes a way of life. Think of either a relationship or an instance in your life where you covered up your true feelings and use it to fill in the blanks below:

"But in order to make it as a _____, I had to learn to wear the image. And I did. I wore it so well that even _____ could not always see through it."

1. To you, what is an image that works like a mask?

2. How does wearing a hard mask to cover up your true feelings make that little girl inside of you feel?

Perfection

> **Highlighted Reading:** "Without even realizing it, I spent the next ten years chasing that flawlessness that had so attracted me as a child, as if it would bring me the fulfillment I longed for. Believing the lies the world tells women about beauty, love, and happiness, I went after perfection until it nearly killed me: the perfect size, the perfect shape, the perfect image, the perfect look, the perfect student, the perfect daughter, the perfect path, the perfect escape. Later, even after I left the business at age twenty-three, I attempted to be the perfect Christian. And that carried into wanting to be the perfect wife who ran a perfect-looking house ...." (pp. 7-8).

3. How intense do you believe is the pressure of perfection on women and girls of this generation?

   Mark an X on the line below.

   Not Intense   Extremely Intense
   _____

4. What is your relationship with perfection? Do you seek it? Do you reject it? In which areas of your life do you long for perfection?

   _____
   _____
   _____
   _____

Read the Webster's dictionary definition of perfection below:

Perfect: being entirely without fault or defect; flawless; satisfying all requirements; corresponding to an ideal standard; lacking in no essential detail.[1]

5. Write in the blanks the relationship between being perfect and being human:

_____

_____

_____

_____

> I'm glad we took the time to identify that little girl inside of you and to touch upon your relationship to image and perfection. We will return to these themes throughout the study and dig deeper into what they mean for you. The next chapter launches us head first into our deepest longing: to be affirmed.
>
> Sadly, for many of us, this first chapter is going to bring up wounds. It seems our greatest wounds come from the "hand of man." Man can steal and destroy the little-girl heart within us…if we let him.

How might God want you to respond to what he's revealed to you today?

_____

_____

_____

Lesson 2
The Longing to Be Affirmed

Read or reread *Girl Perfect*, Chapter 1 "The Perfect Affirmation."

Verse of the Day: "And hope does not disappoint us, because God has poured out his love into our hearts." Romans 5:5a

---

Lie #1:
Your affirmation comes from men.

The Longing:
Affirmation

The longing to be affirmed is the most natural desire of every little girl. We grow up looking to Daddy to affirm us. If he doesn't, we are dejected and broken; if he does, we are given wings to fly. Then over time, things shift, and we begin to look at the boys at school for validation. If we carry the lie in our hearts through high school, college, and into the launch pad of life, man will gain full reign over our self-esteem.

For me, the modeling world was a long series of "stamps of affirmation." Stamped: beautiful. Stamped: ugly. Stamped: wanted. Stamped: not wanted. When those stamps sear themselves onto our hearts, they initially inflict pain; in the long run, they leave scars.

Ultimately, if we believe the lie that we can look to man to fill our longing to be affirmed, we end up sorely disappointed.

The Longing to Be Affirmed

When I first wrestled with how to write my story in a way that applied to all women, I realized that deep inside, we are all looking for the same thing. Whether we are pursuing a career in business or modeling, we are both looking to fill some kind of desire. In this case, the desire is to be affirmed.

Let's review the dictionary definition of *affirmation:* "to validate, confirm; to state positively; to assert, to express dedication to."

1. Where do you fill your longing to be affirmed?

   _____

   _____

2. A longing is a "strong desire or craving." What do you really long for? What do you crave and desire?

   _____

   _____

> **Highlighted Reading:** "I expected him to fill the longings of my heart—the longing for unconditional acceptance and a love that never leaves you. But he was only a boy; he could not fill that place of longing inside me…I thought that by giving him everything, I would *gain*; but there was something I could not touch upon that was irreparably lost" (p. 25).

3. When you find yourself looking to men to fill your deepest longings for love and acceptance, what is the result?

   _____

4. Why do you think men cannot completely fill that longing for affirmation that we have inside of us?

5. Why do you think that giving ourselves away sexually outside of marriage doesn't fill the longing but instead makes it feel greater?

6. If a man (or men) succeeded in giving you the affirmation your little-girl heart desired, use the space below to share about the impact that had on you:

7. If a man (or men) failed to give you the affirmation your little-girl heart desired, please use the space below to open up that wound to God and give it a voice:

_____

_____

_____

I want to encourage you that we all have earthly fathers and a Heavenly Father; earthly princes and a King of Kings. Opening up our hearts to God is always safe, because he knows our wounds already; he is well aware of how humans fall short; and above all, he longs to be our only "Perfect" in a world of imperfection.

Read Psalm 118:8-9

8. Write Psalm 118:8-9 here:

_____

_____

_____

The Twist

The Twist:
To receive affirmation from boys and men,
you must be sexy and sexual.

Some lies have evil twists. The lie that man is the source of our affirmation has a dangerous one. It is: to receive affirmation from boys and men, you must be sexy and sexual. Now we get into a tender arena of our little-girl hearts. We want so badly to be affirmed, and the world tells us that we will get that affirmation by giving our bodies away. This lie can pressure us into doing things with our bodies that are in opposition to the Spirit that lives in us.

> **Highlighted Reading:** "There it was. They would applaud me when I looked like a woman, when I was sexy, when I looked older than I was, and when I was something that, at the moment, I really was not...I was no one's daughter, no one's sister, no one's friend. I was nothing but a thing in a world of things, and my only affirmation came from pleasing them" (pp. 15, 23).

9. What impact do you think this lie has on our little-girl hearts?

10. Give some examples of how the world applauds girls for their sexuality.

11. When we are made to feel we are just things, pieces of flesh to be used for man's pleasure, how does that impact our behavior?

12. How do you think your need to be validated is linked to your sexuality?

13. If you have ever felt pressure to be sexually active, what impact did that have on you?

14. If you chose to be sexually active outside of marriage, did it bring you affirmation? Did it make you feel "dedicated to," validated, thought of positively? How did it make you feel?

15. Have you ever experienced a breakup or saw someone else experience a breakup from a sexually active relationship? What was the end result? Was having sex outside of marriage something you or they regretted or not? Explain.

16. What are your values when it comes to sexuality and purity?

How did you formulate these values? Was God part of that process, and if not, do you wish he had been?

17. If you could turn back time and do things differently, what would you change? Why?

We are so blessed that in Christ all things can be made new, including our purity. I know the topic of this chapter goes straight to our heart of hearts, and for some of us that can be painful. No matter what our experiences have been, naming the lie—that our affirmation comes from men and their use of our sexuality—is very important. Lies can enslave us, making us feel "less than worthy," and preventing us from being who God knows we are meant to be.

18. Let's close this day with truth. Review our verse for the day: "And hope does not disappoint us, because God has poured out his love into our hearts" (Rom. 5:5). Then use the space below to tell God the truth about your need to be affirmed and the right or wrong ways you have sought to fill that need. He is your perfect Father—always—and no matter where you've been or the mistakes you've made, he wants nothing more than to pour out his love into your heart.

How might God want you to respond to what he's revealed to you today?

Lesson 3
Sex

Verse of the Day: "Above all else, guard your heart, for it is the wellspring of life." Proverbs 4:23

It's a common saying that women give sex to receive love and men give love to receive sex. For women, sexual activity outside of marriage stems from our basic desire to be loved. Our world teaches women that they should use their bodies to get the attention, dedication, affection, and acceptance they want. But as my case illustrates, this does not work. Sexual activity outside of marriage left me heartbroken and shamed. On the other hand, when my husband valued, protected, and honored my sexuality before marriage, I received true affirmation—that I was precious and worth waiting for.

One Flesh

> **Highlighted Reading:** "Ultimately, by choosing to do things God's way in a world that scoffs at his protective boundaries, you will find that his blessings will be *yours*. You will also find your affirmation will never hinge on something as fleeting as your sex appeal—it will come from God, a source that never changes and never stops loving you" (p. 29).

1. 1 Corinthians 6:12a says, "Everything is permissible for me—but not everything is beneficial." Can you think of some examples of how this is true when it comes to sexuality?

Read Genesis 2:21-25.

2. What does it mean to you to become "one flesh" with another person?

___

Read 1 Corinthians 6:12-20.

3. How does God describe your body in these verses?

___

4. Recall a time you did not honor God with your body. Really think about this. Why do you think you didn't honor him? What were you in search of?

___

Even if we've asked God for forgiveness and repented or changed, this memory can still be unpleasant for some of us. Nevertheless, it helps us identify specific instances when we lived the lie in search of filling our longing to be affirmed.

5. If you are, or ever were, in sexual sin, this is a chance to ask yourself why. What is leading, or led, you to give your body away? What are, or were, you looking for?

If you never experienced sexual sin or have let it rest in your past, remember that asking yourself why is still important. That's because this study is not just for us but for the next generation and future generations. When I see a movie star or a high school girl or even a middle-aged woman in sexual sin outside of marriage, I know why she's doing it. How can I know? Because I remember.

I remember what I was longing for. I do not judge her because I can see that little girl inside of her longing to be affirmed. I can also see that she believes the lie that she can use her sexuality to receive the affection and approval for which she longs. More than anything, my heart aches for her because she is buying into lie without even realizing it.

6. Why do you think that sexual promiscuity has become so rampant in our culture? What are people looking for?

7. The Message translation of 1 Corinthians 6:12b says, "If I went around doing whatever I thought I could get by with, I'd be a slave to my whims." How can doing whatever feels good at the time result in us becoming a "slave to our whims"?

8. The opposite of slavery is freedom. How can sex within the protective boundaries of marriage bring about real freedom from the lie?

_____

_____

Sexual Abuse and Rape

Sometimes we make ourselves slaves to our own whims; other times we become a slave to someone else's whims. The sad thing about the lie is that it can break our little-girl hearts.

Read 2 Samuel 13:1-22, the story of Tamar.

The four closest men to Tamar all betrayed her: her half-brother, Amnon, who raped her; her cousin Jonadab, who told Amnon how to lure her; her brother Absalom, who told her not to speak of it; and sadly, her father, David, who did nothing about it. How traumatic this must have been for her little-girl heart.

Amnon was driven by lust; Jonadab by deceit; Absalom by fear. Finally, King David had fallen into sexual sin himself with Bathsheba, and he also loved his sons deeply; so he must have been in incredible turmoil on how to handle the rape of his daughter. But he did nothing about it. While he may have known how to shepherd a nation, he failed to shepherd his daughter's heart.

9. When her brother Absalom found out about the rape, what did he tell Tamar to do? (v. 20)

_____

_____

> **Highlighted Reading:** "When a man and woman have sex, they become 'one flesh'; the two become one (Gen.

> 2:24; 1 Cor. 6:12-20). Then, when the relationship ends, and you go one way while he goes the other—whether after one night or ten years—the flesh of your heart can *rip*. If that happens again and again, you may eventually carry the wounds of those relationships into the relationship with your husband—because sexual encounters are actually carried in your body (1 Cor. 6:18)" (p. 28).

10. How would it have been impossible for Tamar not to "take this thing to heart"?

11. Often, when a girl is the target of incest—sex between close relatives—she is told to be quiet about it so as not to bring shame on the family. How does being quiet about it make her wounds even worse?

12. Just to make sure we are perfectly clear on this, answer this: Because there was no witness to her rape (v. 9b), and because she did not file a police report in which they took pictures of her bruises, if there even were any, was it still rape?

    Circle one:

    Yes   No

I appreciate the Bible because it says it like it is: it calls a rape "a rape," whether anyone saw it or not.

Reread 2 Samuel 13:15-19, the throwing out of Tamar.

13. Amnon had believed that he loved Tamar. After he violated her, what happened to that love?

14. After he raped her, Amnon told Tamar to "Get up and get out!" Tamar responded to him that this would be a "greater wrong" than what he had already done to her. His crime destroyed Tamar's chances of marriage because in their day, if she were no longer a virgin, she could not get married. To be violated, abandoned, and alone would bring her great shame. What do verses 18 and 19 say about the state of Tamar's heart after this experience?

Tamar was a victim of the lie that our affirmation comes from men and has to do with our sexuality. In fact, it was her beauty that drew Amnon to her, as it was the beauty of Bathsheba that induced David to commit adultery. Sadly, the whole experience left Tamar's little girl-heart weeping and torn.

15. How can being valued for our outward beauty or for our bodies result in deeply wounding us?

An Issue of the Heart

> **Highlighted Reading:** "By encouraging you to protect your body, God is trying to protect the daughter he loves. Most of all, he wants to protect your heart" (p. 28).

As our verse for the day says, God wants us to guard our hearts above all else. I know what it is to be valued only for my "body." And I know what it is to be valued for more than my body—for my heart too. Lust and love are two very different things: one leaves us shamed and violated; the other brings joy.

Read 1 Corinthians 13:4-7.

16. List the characteristics of love in this passage.

___

___

___

"God is love" (1 John. 4:8). Everything you listed above is what your Father in heaven—the only perfect father you will ever have—wants for you.

Read 1 Corinthians 3:16.

17. What does this verse say about your body?

___

___

Whenever there is a violation in the temple of God, he is consumed with anger about it. In Jesus's day, when there was sin in the temple, he stood up with a whip of cords to drive it out. If you or a loved one has been sexually violated, molested, or raped, I want you to know right here and now that Jesus stood up when he saw that and was consumed with anger. He is the righteous judge and will hold every human being on earth accountable for his actions.

At the same time, just being quiet about it will only lock shame into a deep corridor of your heart. If you have sexual abuse in your past or present, now is the time to deal with it. Yes, it hurts. I know the hurt, and I know the captivity of keeping it locked inside. It took me far too long to speak the truth of my experience, but once I did, it was an essential step in my journey to freedom from the lie that threatened to destroy me.

If there is any truth you feel led to speak here, I want you to do it. It may be the truth that you have been protected from sexual sin and you want to share the praise of that here. Or it may be the truth that you were not protected and you don't want any darkness sealed shut in your little-girl heart because you were told to bury it. Regardless, use this space to speak the truth of your experience, just between you and God:

_____

_____

_____

_____

_____

_____

_____

_____

_____

_____

STUDY GUIDE

Read Isaiah 61:1-3.

18. What did Christ come to do to our hearts?

_____

_____

19. What does he want to replace our ashes with?

_____

20. With what kind of garment will he replace a spirit of despair?

_____

Read Isaiah 61:10 and 62:1-5.

21. When our hearts have been broken and our robes torn, what does God want to clothe us with? (v. 61:10)

_____

I love that in verse 62:1 God says he will not be silent, nor will he "remain quiet," until our righteousness "shines out like the dawn." Our King will not turn his head when our little-girl hearts get torn. As Hebrews 10:30 says, "'Vengeance is mine; I will repay.' And again, 'The Lord will judge his people.'" It is not the will of Jesus to leave Tamar's heart steeped in darkness. It is his will to release her into the light where healing begins, and for her to trust him with her story. When we give our stories to him, he will replace our ashes with beauty, our mourning with gladness, and our despair with praise.

As you meditate on these verses, remember that if you have ever felt "Deserted" or "Desolate," it is the will of God to give you a new name: "My delight is in her" (62:4 NAS). "As a bridegroom rejoices over his bride, so will your God rejoice over you" (62:5). Oh, how he loves you. Let his affirmation wash over you and fill your heart.

Nothing torn within us is beyond God's ability to mend; nothing destroyed is beyond his ability to restore.

> How might God want you to respond to what he's revealed to you today?
>
> _____
>
> _____
>
> _____

Close this day in prayer.

Lesson 4
Shame

Verse of the Day: "Those who look to him are radiant; their faces are never covered with shame." Psalm 34:5

In our culture, shame is interwoven with misused sexuality. This dates back to the early scholars who considered Eve a seductress who used her wily ways to tempt her husband into eating the apple. The truth is, however, Adam chose to eat it, and it had nothing to do with Eve's sexuality! The fruit looked good to him too, and he ate—period (Gen. 3:6). After that, shame entered the garden (Gen. 3:10). Prior to that time, there was no shame (Gen. 2:25).

Today we still carry the shame that was placed on Eve. If a man sins, it is still often blamed on women's sexuality instead of man's sinful nature. History has taught us that our sexuality is somehow our fault, therefore tying woman's sexuality to sinfulness. Of course, this is wrong thinking and has been quite damaging to women. But here's the truth that sets us free from that backward philosophy: All that God created is good, and that includes women's sexuality! (Gen. 1:31) Our sexuality is what brings forth new life into the world (our children), and it is what unites us to our husbands. This is all good; in fact, it is wonderful.

How women—and men—treat female sexuality is the key to whether it is used for good or for evil. We saw this in the case of Tamar. If our sexuality is protected, nurtured, and valued, it is good. If it is exploited or devalued, it is evil.

Because sexual sin is carried in the body, women store the blame of sexual transgression within them, often burying it deep in the heart. If we bury it, we carry it.

If buried, sexual sin has the potential to impact the most private and vital areas of our lives with shame. As Beth Moore says, "Shame is Satan's stamp of approval."[2] Whether the shame is justified or not—on the one hand, we have sinned sexually, or on the other hand, we carry the shame of someone else's sexual sin—the bottom line is women carry shame within their hearts, and it is often linked to the use or misuse of their sexuality. So let's unpack this one today, making sure that we do not walk forward carrying the shame of what is, and truly can be, behind us.

Keep in mind—as I implore you throughout the study—that if you do not struggle with sexual shame (because you have no sexual sin in your past and carry no shame regarding your sexuality, which makes you quite rare), please do not assume this study guide is not for you. In your neighborhood, community, church, school, and workplace, there are countless women and girls who carry far too much shame. Those of us who are free and healed must offer them Christ, who will wash away their sin and replace it with wholeness and purity. It is up to us to help restore the daughters of the King.

Sex and Sin

1. We established in the book that your sexuality is not a shameful thing in itself. Using the line below, write an X to show how much or little you truly believe that:

    My Sexuality Is Not Sinful   My Sexuality Is Sinful

2. Do you believe that sex outside of marriage is sin? Keep in mind our generation finds loopholes for this; many do "everything but" the sex act and say they are pure. So, to be more specific, do you believe sexual activity in which you completely share your body with another outside of marriage is sin? Put an X on the line below to show how much you believe it. (Be real with what you really think—not what your mother or daughter thinks you should think!)

    Sex Outside of   Sex Outside of
    Marriage Is Sin   Marriage Is Not Sin

3. Hebrews 13:4a says, "Marriage should be honored by all, and the marriage bed kept pure." What do you think this means?

Read Ephesians 5:25-31.

4. At what point is a man supposed to become one flesh with a woman?

5. What is the woman called in verse 31? Circle one:

   His girlfriend
   His date
   His acquaintance to whom he is sexually attracted
   His wife

I apologize if this seems a bit elementary, but the truth is the average teen and twenty-something in and outside of church is not convinced that sex is for marriage only, so we are obligated to spell it out! This also comes with the understanding that when I was a teen, I had no idea what sin was. So I have no judgment; only understanding.

Nevertheless, from the point that we realize God's true design for sex within marriage, if we are followers of Christ, we are held to God's standard. If we commit sexual sin, the Holy Spirit will convict our hearts. We may try to deny the conviction, but it will remain until we repent or change. When sex is practiced outside God's pure design, there will be shame, fear, and confusion.

There are two sides to the coin of shame: 1) shame instilled in us from a perpetrator, in which case we were innocent victims and 2) shame instilled in us as a result of our own decision to commit sin. Because so many women and girls have been sexually abused, I want to put that first type of shame to rest where it belongs. Then we will look at our own shame and what Christ has to say about it.

Shame on Whom?

6. Let's take a quick journey through the Psalms to see what they say about shame. Read the following verses and write next to them what they say about the shame of those who hurt the innocent:

    Psalm 25:1-3:

    Psalm 40:14-15:

    Psalm 71:24:

Read Psalm 132:18.

7. Write Psalm 132:18 here:

8. What does that verse say to Tamar, me, and you?

It's been done! Past, present, and future—if you put your hope in God, those that have shamed you will be put to their own shame. The shame is not yours to carry. It's between them and God. Do we still need to forgive them? Yes. The key to forgiveness is handing them over to your King. Let him crown you and mend your robe. And let him clothe the ones who hurt you in shame. He can handle them just fine. Trust God with those who have hurt you, and do not carry their shame. That belongs to them alone.

Shame on Me

In many of our cases, the shame of our sexual sin is our shame. We brought it on by believing the lie. We believed that our longing to be affirmed would be filled by man; and, we believed that giving away our sacred sexuality was a formula for filling our longing to be loved.

9. Read the following verses and write next to them what they say about your shame:

   Isaiah 54:4-8:

   Isaiah 61:7:

   Romans 10:11:

10. Take a look at our verse for the day: "Those who look to him are radiant; their faces are never covered with shame" (Ps. 34:5). What does that say to you?

Hebrews 12:2 says, "Let us fix our eyes on Jesus, the author and perfecter of our faith, who for the joy set before him endured the cross, scorning its shame, and sat down at the right hand of the throne of God." Scorn means "to reject or dismiss as contemptible or unworthy." In other words, Jesus eliminated the author of shame, Satan himself, on the cross, removing the shame from our faces forever. No matter how it took root in us, shame has been dismissed, rejected, rebuked! So we cannot take one step forward into the radiant life while we are still carrying it.

Nailing the Shame Where It Belongs

11. I want you to make Hebrews 12:2 personal. What happened to your shame on the cross?

12. According to the Book of John, the last words Jesus breathed on the cross before he gave up his spirit were: "It is finished" (19:30). What does it mean to you to know that after he took all your shame on the cross, Jesus returned to the Father and "sat down" at his right hand?

The most important thing we can do with any sin—specifically sexual sin, abuse, or an unhealthy dependence on male affirmation—is to accept Christ's death on the cross as a message of undying love for us and a confirmation of our incredible value. We can nail our shame to the cross for good.

When he died for us, he "became" our shame so that we would not have to shoulder the burden of sin, regret, and bitterness any longer. He dismissed shame from us, "as far as the east is from the west" (Ps. 103:12).

13. On the cross, Jesus stood in the gap for us, separating us from shame forever. Draw a sketch of that below, just to make it visual for you.

Remember, after the Fall, God cursed Satan to eat ashes for the rest of his days. God's will is not for us to keep those ashes on our head, as Tamar did. Instead, God's will is to make us as resplendent as the crowns that we wear.

Only he can fill the longings of our little-girl hearts: knowing this begins the journey. Thank you for diving in with me. It's going to be a remarkable swim.

How might God want you to respond to what he's revealed to you today?

_____

_____

_____

Lesson 5
Made New

Verse of the Day: "You have stolen my heart, my sister, my bride; you have stolen my heart." Song of Songs 4:9a

Well, girlfriend, we sure jumped into it, didn't we? When I gave my mother the first draft of *Girl Perfect*, she read it with many tears, as you might imagine. When she called me, she gasped, "Oh, Jenny! Chapter One!"

"I know, Mom," I said. My eyes still fill with tears as I recall the pain and wonder in her voice. I'm sure her gasp came from knowing that my little-girl heart had been torn, and I had been afraid to speak of it. Of course, as a mother, that tore hers too. But I cannot help believing her gasp also came from joy at the restored bride I became.

We treasure the vision of our wedding days in our hearts. I can picture mine: preparing myself during the weeks ahead of time with beauty treatments and exercise; choosing the cake, the colors, the flowers; the rehearsal with my bridesmaids, my friends, and my husband-to-be, his companions at his side.

My mother was with me when I chose the gown—the first one I tried on was the "one." Of course, I tried on many more, but ended up with the first—the bodice beaded with pearls and lace, a satin band that lay across my chest. The white veil was translucent and fell softly down my back. I wore pearls that day. Oh, the joy of emerging from my room of preparation and walking out into that glorious day! The sun basked the garden in light, casting golden beads of beauty between the cascading willow trees that surrounded the white gazebo where we married.

The whole family was there, of course. Shane's mother, Linda, couldn't possibly contain the tears. Shane was a prodigal: he left home in search of freedom and ended up wallowing in the worst of mud. His family never thought they would see this day. Christ returned us both from our shame; he stood in the gap for us and gave us new lives.

Walking Down the Aisle

Read Song of Songs 1:15-2:7.

The Song of Songs is both a picture of God's love for his people and a picture of married love and sex.

1. What do you think it means here that we should not "arouse or awaken love until it so desires"?

    _____

    _____

    _____

Read Song of Songs 2:8-13.

This romantic depiction of love is set in a garden. I love that it says, "The winter is past; the rains are over and gone," and we see a description of the full bloom of spring. Jesus is the living water that washes away our sin and cleanses us and restores us, so that we can enjoy married sex as God designed. In the words of Hosea 6:3, "Let us acknowledge the LORD; let us press on to acknowledge him. As surely as the sun rises, he will appear; he will come to us like the winter rains, like the spring rains that water the earth." Joel 2:23 says, "Be glad, O people of Zion, rejoice in the LORD your God, for he has give you the autumn rains in righteousness. He sends you abundant showers…"

His blood literally washes us clean and refreshes us to be renewed in every way.

Leave a bookmark in Song of Songs and turn to Genesis.

STUDY GUIDE

Read Genesis 15:6.

2. What does this verse say our righteousness comes from?

Faith is credited to us as righteousness (Rom. 4:9). Righteousness, according to the dictionary, is "always behaving according to a moral code; correct; justifiable." We have all sinned and fallen short of the glory of God. None of us has "always behaved!" The very thought of it makes me laugh. It's impossible for human beings to be righteous on their own.

Christ is the only Perfect. And he does a perfect thing for us through the cross.

Read Isaiah 53:3-12.

3. Write verse 11 below:

Review Isaiah 61:3 again.

4. Write the last sentence of verse 3 below, beginning with, "They will be called…"

That's right, my friend! The righteous one died for us so we could be called righteous, so that he could plant us "as oaks of righteousness" for the "display of his splendor."

The Wedding Gown

Review Isaiah 61:10-11.

5. With what kind of robe does the Lord dress us?

   _____

Keep your finger in Isaiah, and turn to the Psalms.

Read Psalm 37:5-6.

6. What happens when we commit our way to the Lord, no matter where we've been?

   _____

   _____

   _____

Flip back to Isaiah and read verse 45:8.

7. When he "rains down" righteousness on us, what springs up?

   _____

I used to always try to shower to wash away the hurt. Now Jesus rains on me and clothes me with himself. I could just shout for joy. In fact, I think I will! You should too! He rains down righteousness and springs forth praise. Praise him!

Recently I was told that the name Jenny means "the grace of God." Jenny is the name everyone called me when I was a little girl. Now my friends call me Jen. I had never heard that definition for Jenny, so I looked it up. The actual meaning is "white, fair, smooth," which thrilled me just as much. My friend, when you give your heart to Jesus, he can restore that little girl inside of you who was once pure as the fallen snow; he can make you new and clothe you in a white gown. He can take away your shame and make you resplendent with beauty.

Now, turn back to your bookmark in Song of Songs.

Read Song of Songs 4:9-15.

8. How does God see you?

9. To what does he compare you?

We are precious to God, and so is our purity. It is a garden "locked up" until love awakens it. It grieves God's heart when our sexuality is not protected as sacred. But when it is valued and treated with love and care, we become "like a garden fountain," and from us springs forth life in abundance.

Truth in the Face of Lies

God hates lies, for they come from "the father of lies" (John 8:44). God is truth; he cannot lie. We can be free from the lies that enslave us by speaking truth to them. The Word of God is truth. It is the sword that will slay the evil one.

Our first lie was: "Your affirmation comes from men." Its dangerous twist was: "To receive affirmation from boys and men, you must be sexy and sexual."

10. Why is this a lie? Really think about your answer.

Truth #1
Perfect affirmation comes
from God alone.

When we are looking for affirmation, we are really in search of someone to tell us we are good enough. Man cannot do that for us; only God can. Perfect affirmation comes from God alone. Only he can fill that longing in our little-girl hearts to be affirmed. And when we receive the cross with faith, he clothes us in robes of his righteousness and teaches us how sacred and beautiful we are in his eyes.

11. The longing is to be affirmed. The lie is that you can get that longing filled from the world. The truth is God wants to fill it. Use the space below to write what you've learned about your own need for affirmation and list some practical ways you can allow God to fill that longing for you.

How might God want you to respond to what he's revealed to you today?

_____

_____

_____

Close your day in prayer. There is a new longing we will explore in the next lessons. See you there!

Girl Perfect Readings

Chapter 2—The Perfect Acceptance:
Girls, Jealousy, and the Comparison Game

Chapter 3—The Perfect Image:
Getting Real

Lessons

6: Jealousy and Comparisons

7: The Domino Effect

8: Eyes of Grace

9: Unveiled

10: Taking off the Masks

Lesson 6
Jealousy and Comparisons

Read or reread *Girl Perfect*, Chapter 2, "The Perfect Acceptance." Verse of the Day: "A heart at peace gives life to the body, but envy rots the bones." Proverbs 14:30

Lie #2
Looking at other women/girls
shows how you measure up.

The Longing:
Acceptance

I love sharing the stories about the models' apartments. They were such a bird's-eye view into the nature of women. Our apartments truly were revolving doors through which girl after girl after girl cycled, being promised that in that grand world of modeling she would find all that her heart longed for—love, peace, success, hope, and a future.

It was truly disheartening to see Tina degenerate the way she did. When I first came to Milan, she greeted me at the door, light on her feet, eyes sparkling and full of hope. Laughter naturally bubbled out of her. While I was chasing the dream with a vengeance, Tina was more relaxed. She could laugh at herself and be silly and not care what anyone thought. But rejection chips away at the innocent hope of our little-girl hearts. Rejection after rejection after rejection… after a while, our hearts crumble until it's not so easy to laugh anymore.

The last time Tina exited through that revolving door, I'm sure the bitter cold, dreary Milanese day made her all the more depressed.

Milan had failed her, and she had failed Milan. To this day I wonder whether she went back to university, as she sometimes talked about doing. I hope she did, but more than that, I hope she found out she was beautiful and lovable just as she was, her lopsided shoulder, flat chest, and all.

Too bad I didn't know the truth back then. I was so concerned about clutching onto the measuring stick of comparison, charting myself against other girls, thinking I had to get on top, that I couldn't see them or myself for who we really were.

Girls, Girls, Girls!

Girls, girls, girls! If only we could see each other through God's eyes. Girls can be so jealous, so cruel, so catty, and so conniving that our deepest wounds can come from one another.

Be careful while you do this study to check your masquerade at the door. Just as we can cover up the way men have hurt us, so we have become experts at projecting a perfect image with other women. A lot of us are nice to women and girls on the outside, but in our hearts...oh, yes, we are comparing; we are jealous; we are afraid of what makes others more bright and beautiful; and we are judging. So be real in the days to come. Be real.

The Acceptance Factor

> **Highlighted Reading:** "We ultimately want to be chosen *over* the other girl while at the same time not be rejected by her" (p. 37).

Let's review the definition of acceptance: "to be received favorably; to be approved of; to be endured without protest."

1. How important is it to you to be accepted by your peers? Make an X on the line below to show how vital this is in

terms of your value and self-esteem. Keep in mind that it is very normal to desire acceptance from other girls and women.

Not Important   Very Important

> **Highlighted Reading:** "The dynamic in our apartment is dicey: we are all young and looking for something—this unites us. But ... we are competing with each other—this divides us" (p. 36).

2. Among girls and women, what unites?

3. What divides?

4. We all long to be accepted as we are. But there is something in the female makeup that judges other women, almost the moment we see them. We size them up; we evaluate them by their appearance; we compare. Why do you think we do that?

The Rejection Factor

5. How does rejection affect you?

6. Using the space below, make a list of your experiences with acceptance and rejection as they relate to your relationships with girls/women.

   Acceptance   Rejection

7. Which one of those that you listed had the deepest impact on you and why?

Jealousy and the Comparison Game

Read James 4:1-2.

8. What causes jealousy?

Read Galatians 5:16-26.

9. Some of us think of jealousy and envy as just natural human tendencies. What do these verses say about jealousy and envy?

> **Highlighted Reading:** "The jealousy, competition, and comparisons between the girls created a never-ending, exhausting cycle, and we *all* came up lacking for the toll it took on us" (p. 42).

10. How do jealousy and comparisons create a vicious cycle that takes a toll on you?

11. Reread our verse for the day: "A heart at peace gives life to the body, but envy rots the bones" (Prov. 14:30). I described in the book how Tina, Val, and I all physically disintegrated from the pressure to be perfect and the comparison game of the modeling world. How do you think envy can actually have a physical effect on you?

12. How do you think having a heart at peace can also be reflected physically?

_____

_____

_____

> **Highlighted Reading:** "Every girl there was checking out the legs of the other girls, summing up on a scale of 1 to 10 how she looked in the dress. For some reason it made me feel better when I saw the cottage cheese on the back of one girl's thighs, but worse when another had cleavage spilling from the neckline... Comparisons, comparisons, comparisons, comparisons. I could not escape them; even when I didn't want to be compared, even when I was content with being myself, when I felt like our differences truly made us unique and weren't a cause for jealousy, still, the comparisons were there" (pp. 39,45).

13. Do you ever feel better when you "compare better"? Place a line on the X below to represent your answer:

    Yes   No

    _____

14. Does it ever make you feel worse when another girl/woman is smarter, prettier, more talented? Place an X on the line to represent your answer:

    Yes   No

    _____

15. Explain your answers:

16. How can using other girls/women as measuring sticks of your worth be damaging to your own sense of worth?

17. How can using other girls/women as measuring sticks of your worth be damaging to your friendships?

It is always good to explore the effects of the lie before we move on to the truth. As you close this day, pray about any feelings of jealousy, bitterness, or low self-worth you may have as a result of believing the lie. Give God your little-girl heart, even if you're ninety years old. We've all been hurt. Share with him how your list of rejections made you feel and resolve to surround yourself with Christ-like acceptance, extending it in turn to others.

How might God want you to respond to what he's revealed to you today?

Lesson 7
The Domino Effect

Verse of the Day: "Jesus straightened up and asked her, 'Woman... has no one condemned you?' 'No one, sir,' she said. 'Then neither do I condemn you,' Jesus declared." John 8:10-11

The comparison game has a domino effect: one sin leads to another and another. We are going to explore that effect today in hopes that we will dodge the pitfalls of jealousy and comparison. When we believe the lie that "looking at other women and girls shows how we measure up," we fall into its trap, with negative self-esteem hindering our God-given callings. We end up bruised and beaten down or even worse: we bruise and beat down other women out of fear that they are better than we are. Such was the story of two men chosen by God to spread the gospel message.

In Acts 13:2, we see that God set apart Barnabas and Saul (also called Paul) for the work to which God had called them. Over the course of the next chapter, we see them traveling and sharing the good news of Jesus Christ. Some people wanted to hear more; others responded in fear and envy.

Jealousy Leads To...

Read Acts 13:38-45, the experience of Paul and Barnabas.

In the same way people responded to Jesus, some Jews engaged with Paul and Barnabas very positively, while others had extremely negative reactions.

1. Fill in the blank:

    When the Jews saw all the crowds who were drawn to the message of Paul and Barnabas, they were filled with _____.

2. How did their jealousy manifest itself?

Read Acts 13:46-52.

3. Compare the Gentiles' reaction to Paul and Barnabas to the reaction of the Jews of high standing:

4. How were Paul and Barnabas affected by the people's acceptance and rejection? (vv. 51-52.)

Read Acts 14:1-20, the continued journey of Paul and Barnabas.

5. What did Paul and Barnabas say when the people wanted to worship them? (v. 15.)

6. What other emotions and actions did the Jews' jealousy lead to?

7. How did jealousy affect them on a spiritual level?

STUDY GUIDE

8. How did Paul and Barnabas respond to the Jews' mistreatment?

The apostles followed the exact pattern of Jesus: when people accepted the message, they preached it; when people rejected the message, they preached it! The ability to "shake the dust from our feet" comes from knowing the truth and being set free by it: our level of acceptance doesn't come from man, but from God.

Clearly, jealousy can prevent us from receiving a message that God wants us to hear. It can also make us so angry that we try to stop God's work.

> **Highlighted Reading:** "Comparisons fuel jealousy; jealousy fuels hatred; hatred fuels anger; and anger, in turn, fuels fear" (p. 40).

9. In the space below, write how this domino effect works:

Judgement

One of the main reasons why religious people hated Jesus was because his perfection convicted them of their own sinful hearts, and they weren't open to dealing with their hearts! They didn't want to see themselves in light of a perfect God. This hatred led them to take judgment into their own hands and condemn Jesus on the cross.

Since we are being real here, let's acknowledge that women and girls can be extremely judgmental of one another, and that judging others actually makes us the ugly ones.

As one who has felt judged, betrayed, and condemned by others, I empathize with the judged a lot more than I do with the ones who point fingers.

> **Highlighted Reading:** "'You can't be too perfect, or we'll hate you. On the other hand, if you aren't perfect enough, we'll nail you to the wall'" (p. 46).

10. Have you ever disliked or even hated someone because you thought she was too perfect? Why?

___

___

___

11. Have you ever felt disliked by someone else because she thought you were too perfect? If so, explain how that made you feel:

___

___

___

12. Have you ever felt "nailed to the wall" by other girls/women? How did that make you feel?

___

STUDY GUIDE

_____

_____

Read John 8:1-11, the story of the woman caught in adultery.

13. Why did the religious leaders bring the woman caught in adultery into the temple courts and question Jesus about her?

   Circle one:
   a. To show their love for her
   b. So Jesus could forgive her
   c. To trap Jesus
   d. To have a basis for accusing him C and D

14. Explain the meaning of this statement: "If anyone of you is without sin, let him be the first to throw a stone at her" (John. 8:7).

   _____

   _____

   _____

> **Highlighted Reading:** "The hypocrites pointed their fingers at the woman caught in adultery because that took the focus off themselves. Let's find the girl who messes up and make it public—so everyone will look at *her* and not us" (p. 47).

15. How does judging others conveniently take the focus off ourselves?

   _____

   _____

Read Romans 2:1-4.

16. Explain what these verses mean.

Read Romans 3:23.

17. Write Romans 3:23 below:

Read 1 Corinthians 4:3-5.

18. Through whom did Paul meet his need for acceptance?

19. How do you think God feels about us having a superior attitude toward others?

20. How do you think God feels about us believing the lie that we are somehow inferior to others?

Finally, read 1 Corinthians 4:9-13.

21. Like Christ, the apostles experienced profound rejection and condemnation from man. How does Paul inspire us to respond when others judge us?

> **Highlighted Reading:** "If [Jesus]—being perfect in every way—looks at imperfect people with eyes of acceptance, shouldn't you and I begin to look at others this way too?... If he who was without sin is not going to throw a stone at us, maybe we need to drop our rocks" (p. 48).

22. What does it mean to "drop our rocks"?

23. How have you been hurt by comparisons and judgment?

24. Is there someone you are judging or have judged? Open up about that here.

_____

_____

If we hold on with a vise grip to the right to judge others, it will squeeze the life out of our hearts. The domino effect that begins with the lie can end up rotting us from the inside out. But if we hold on with a vise grip to the truth of who we are in God's eyes, it changes the way we look at the women and girls in our midst.

25. To close this day of study, read the passage below and fill your name in the blanks.

> "God made you, _____, and he knows that at the very core of your heart you just want to be accepted as you are. But he also knows that what you are longing for can't be filled by what the world has to offer. When Jesus went to the cross for us, in essence, he said, 'I accept you, _____!' in neon lights, with letters written in his own blood and tears. He said, '_____, I don't want your sins to separate you from a holy God anymore. Everyone falls short of perfect; all stumble. I want you to be free from comparisons._____, I want you to be free to be the girl God made'" (pp. 48-49).

How might God want you to respond to what he's revealed to you today?

_____

_____

_____

Close your time today with prayer.

Lesson 8
Eyes of Grace

Verse of the Day: "We love because he first loved us." 1 John 4:19

In studying real beauty in God's eyes, I've discovered that beauty has a lot more to do with how we look at others than with our own appearance. Most women and girls wrestle on and off throughout their lives to earn an outward stamp of approval through their appearance or their work. But when we look to the world to fill the longings of our little-girl hearts, our hearts get deprived of the real nourishment they need.

Today I want to take a close look at something that makes us beautiful from the inside out. The best way to do that is to sharply contrast it to ugliness. Because judgment and condemnation are so closely linked in the domino effect, we will study condemnation today as the final tile that falls, burying our little-girl hearts in the darkest of pits.

Say a prayer before you begin, that God would give you spiritual eyes to see the subjects of today's lesson. They are essential in your journey to freedom.

Condemnation and Love

It's amazing how the domino effect works. It starts with something as natural as the comparison game, which everyone does. But then, if left unchecked, comparisons lead to jealousy, then hatred, anger, fear, judgment, and finally, condemnation. To condemn is to "make a judicial pronouncement stating what punishment must be imposed upon a person found guilty of a crime, especially in the case of a death sentence." Sounds just like what the religious people did to the woman caught in adultery.

Certainly they didn't act in a way that drew that woman to come to their church, did they? If I were her, I would have run screaming from their church. But Jesus drew her by his love.

Sons of Hell

In Matthew 23, Jesus let us know what he really thinks about the religious people such as those who brought the woman caught in adultery to the temple in John 8.

Read Matthew 23:15.

1. What does he call the Pharisees and teachers of the law? Circle all that apply:

   Sons of the Most High
   Sons of hell
   Hypocrites
   His disciples

Read Matthew 23:27-28.

2. How can whitewashed tombs be like masks? What were their masks covering up?

   _____

   _____

   _____

Read Matthew 23:33.

3. What does he call religious people here?

   _____

   _____

4. What burning question does he ask them?

_____

_____

Jesus hated hypocrisy, can you tell?

Read John 8:31-47 very carefully. We will be referring to this passage a lot in the coming lessons.

5. To whom is Jesus talking? (v. 31)

_____

Jesus was talking to the people who actually believed in him. That means they were what today we call Christians. He told them that they needed to be set free, which made no sense to them because they didn't consider themselves enslaved by anyone. But Jesus point-blank told them they were not sons of Abraham, because they didn't do what Abraham did.

6. Instead, what did Jesus say to them in verse 41? Write it here:

_____

_____

They tried to tell him that God was their Father, but he rebuked them.

Read John 8:44 again, carefully.

7. Who is Jesus saying is their father? (v. 44)

_____

8. What is the native language of the devil? (v. 44)

_____

9. What is Jesus's native language? (v. 45)

10. What do the children of God do? (v. 42)

11. What do the children of the devil do? (v. 41)

This one is a killer. Here we have believers being called children of the devil. Jesus used the words snakes and brood of vipers to describe them.

In Revelation 12:9-10, the devil is called "that ancient serpent," "Satan, who leads the whole world astray," and "the accuser of our brothers, who accuses them before God day and night." So when we are pointing the finger at other people, looking for a basis of accusing them, we are doing what the devil does.

And according to John 8:41-44, when we do what the devil does, we are his children.

No wonder Jesus warned the accusers that they too could be in hell and called them "sons of hell!" (Matt. 23:15). Ouch! That one blazes like a raging fire!

So if you are a Christian, you are not free from judgment when you judge others (Rom. 2:1-3). I implore religious people: get over yourself; drop your rocks; and do not wear a mask to cover up your sinful heart. Children of the devil are known by their condemnation. True followers of Christ are known by our love.

12. Stop for a moment and pray. Then use the space below to respond to what you've learned so far today:

Daughters of God

Read John 13:33-34.

13. Who does Jesus call the people he is addressing?

14. Write verses 34 and 35 below:

Just to make sure we are clear on this, when we judge, we are daughters of hell. When we love, we are daughters of God.

Read Romans 8:1-3.

There is no condemnation for those of us who are in Christ because Jesus set us free from condemnation on the cross. There he "condemned sin in sinful man" (8:3). So it is neither our right nor our role to judge, but only to love as he first loved us.

Read 1 John 4:7-12 and 19-21.

15. What is God's command and desire for us when it comes to our treatment of other girls and women?

16. If we hate others, what does John say about us?

Finally, read Galatians 5:6b (the second sentence).

17. This is one of my very favorite and life-defining verses. Write it here:

18. How can you apply this verse to your everyday life?

Eyes of Grace

> **Highlighted Reading:** "When you see other people through the eyes of the cross, suddenly, at the core, we are all the same" (p. 49).

19. Explain what this statement means to you:

> **Highlighted Reading:** "The eyes of God are the eyes of acceptance despite your imperfections, despite your shortcomings, despite your mistakes. The eyes of God are the eyes of grace. As a girl who follows God, or at least searches for him, you must take on eyes of grace" (p. 48).

20. What are "eyes of grace"?

Wow! We've learned a lot so far. Let's end this day of study with truth. As Jesus said, "The truth shall set you free." If we would only admit that at times we've been slaves to the lie! Lies can bind us and keep us from becoming all that God wants us to be.

Our second lie was: Looking at other women/girls shows how you measure up. Our second truth, which replaces that lie, comes straight from the voice of Christ: "I give you a perfect acceptance. Now you give it to others."

Truth #2
Christ says, "I give you a perfect acceptance.
Now you give it to others."

Take that truth to heart! Impress it upon your heart. Learning to look at everyone we see through the eyes of the cross can change our lives forever. At the cross, you can find a love for yourself and for others that you cannot find anywhere else. Jesus's desire for every child of his is to see through his eyes—eyes that love.

Real beauty stems from real grace. Believe it, and live it.

> How might God want you to respond to what he's revealed to you today?
>
> _____
>
> _____
>
> _____

Lesson 9
Unveiled

Read or reread *Girl Perfect*, Chapter 3, "The Perfect Image."

Verse of the Day: "But whenever anyone turns to the Lord, the veil is taken away...And we, who with unveiled faces all reflect the Lord's glory, are being transformed into his likeness." 2 Corinthians 3:16, 18a

---

Lie #3
If something looks good on the outside,
it is good on the inside.

The Longing:
To be Received

We see this lie everywhere we look—on social media, the internet, in magazines, movies, on television, in churches, sports, schools, and workplaces. The lie tricks us into believing that what we see on the outside is what is real, that image reflects reality. The effect of this lie on girls and women is that we are taught to wear masks, making everything look pretty on the outside while covering up unhappiness, pain, or turmoil within. The world teaches us that it favors image over reality. We, in turn, fear realness. If we are real, we fear we will likely be rejected. So we choose the façade as a means of gaining acceptance.

Because we live in a world of masks, it is extraordinarily refreshing to meet a real, honest, authentic woman. When we meet one, we take a deep breath. Immediately, we like her. When we ask how she is, she tells the truth; she gives us permission to tell the truth ourselves. She teaches us that realness is a soft, cool breeze in an otherwise stuffy room.

If you haven't figured this out yet, both the book *Girl Perfect* and this study are founded on the truth that being real is good. That God—and people—actually appreciate and pursue authenticity. One reason why it took me so long to bring the book to life via publishing is that I was terrified of the real. I was afraid to face what was real in my life and to share it so openly with the world. It wasn't until my love for you as a reader became stronger than my fear of getting real that I was actually able to publish my story. As 1 John 4:18 says, "There is no fear in love. But perfect love drives out fear."

As I will say often, the only thing perfect on earth is the love of God. His perfect love for me drove out the fear; it made being real with you more important than worrying about your image of me. My image comes from how I look in God's eyes, not yours.

An interesting thing that happened after the book went to print was that I received—and continue to receive—letters from women and girls around the world, pouring out pain and fears that they had hidden behind masks for years. Often their husbands, boyfriends, parents, friends, and children had no idea what they felt beneath the surface, yet these women wrote to me. I kept asking myself, "Why me? Why don't they go to their pastors? A counselor? A friend? Why are they contacting me, of all people"?

Over time I realized that my realness in *Girl Perfect* gives people permission to be real themselves. I am a safe harbor for anyone who is hurting because I am so honest about the hurt. They know I'm not going to judge them; they know I'm going to relate; they know I believe in getting real.

Recently I received a letter from a German woman named Patricia who had a skin disease when she was a teenager. She sent me a picture of herself in the midst of the illness, and it was terrible. The disease looked like my problems with cystic acne times five hundred. From experience I know that a woman's dignity is in no way related to the state of her skin. Nevertheless, I felt deep empathy for her because our world tells her that her appearance is congruent to her dignity.

More horrific than the state of her skin was that her father, teachers, friends, and community ridiculed, tormented, and rejected her on account of her appearance. Her father cruelly shut her out of his life, claiming she brought him shame and embarrassment, and refused any acknowledgment of Patricia's severe emotional distress. Almost unimaginable, her high school teacher repetitively mocked her, even forcing her to stand in front of the class while lambasting her with insults.

The most grievous thing Patricia shared with me is that in German, the word ugly means "hated." Due to no fault of her own, her self-image and life were shattered by the lie that perfect equals beautiful and beautiful equals loved. Of course, the flip side to the lie is that imperfect equals ugly and ugly equals hated.

"If something looks good on the outside, it must be good on the inside," the world lies. It follows that, "If something looks bad on the outside, it must be bad on the inside." A perfect image is loved and applauded; and in Patricia's case, an imperfect image is hated and despised.

Patricia used words like *ugly, ashamed, worthless, guilty, hated, hopeless, isolated, and invisible* to describe how she felt. The overwhelming emotional effect of her skin disease on her was completely ignored by her family. Her father refused to discuss her depression and trauma, and out of sheer desperation, her mother lied to people, saying they had a happy family life and that her daughter was doing well, even though in truth Patricia's depression had led her to drop out of university. Patricia was forced to pretend she was living a life she wasn't really living. Everyone focused on her skin rather than her soul, and no one ever asked her how she felt. The mask-wearing left her shattered, miserable, and screaming inside.

Having believed all her life—due to the philosophy of her father and teachers—that Jesus was just a symbol and God could not be known, she had nowhere to turn. But one day she came across a Bible study that explained the gospel and spoke about the resurrection. She began to pray and felt incredible comfort. She began to stand up for herself and to realize the truth—that her life had not been happy at all. She found help, underwent therapy, and for the first time in her life experienced the incredible relief of talking freely about what happened. Her road to healing began with hope that there was a God who saw her heart and loved her beyond the image. God saw through the masks she was forced to wear and reached into the depths of her heart and met her there.

Even though she is now physically healed and spiritually saved, this young woman is still deeply wounded by the world's rejection and is still in search of God's plan for her life. Because no one supported her during her depression, she has no education and as of this writing, no way to support herself, which has caused tremendous turmoil. In other words, it's still not perfect, so we might as well not pretend like it is. But God is perfecting her and is using her life, and that is the good news.

Image. Masks. Realness. These are the topics of the next two days. I look forward to unpacking these concepts with you as we tackle the formidable impact they have on this generation.

Image

1. When you see the word image, what do you think of?

_____

_____

Let's review our definition of *image:* "an imitation of a person or thing; a representation, likeness, impression or conception of oneself; an illusion."

> **Highlighted Reading:** "We live in a world that promotes exterior beauty above vulnerability. The more perfect the image, the more applause it receives" (p. 61).

2. Give some examples from our culture where this proves to be true:

> **Highlighted Reading:** "The world is much more interested in image than it is in reality. It wants to believe that the girl in the picture is as satisfied as she looks. The world doesn't *really* want to know that the girl in the picture is no longer the girl in the picture—she has lost her innocence, her faith in people, her money, her hope, and her security..." (p. 59).

3. Do you agree? Disagree? Why or why not?

We all long to be loved and valued for more than the outward appearance; we all long for someone to look deep within our souls and appreciate what lies beneath the surface. The longing is real for all of us. And the truth is we all want to be beautiful. God's heart cries for us to know that we are. His eyes look upon the women he created and weep when they believe the lie that they have to measure up to the *image of the world* instead of embracing that they are his *image in the world*.

His Image in the World

Read Genesis 1:27.

4. What does this verse say about your image?

Read Colossians 1:15-20.

5. What does this say about Christ's image?

Read Colossians 3:9-10.

6. What image does God desire to renew us into?

Through faith in Christ, we are supposed to die to our old image and be renewed in his image. But that doesn't just happen automatically. The veil over our hearts has to be removed first.

Read 2 Corinthians 3:13-18 and I will explain what I mean.

The veil Paul is talking about here is the one Moses wore when he descended from Mount Sinai with the Ten Commandments. Moses was the only man who ever spoke face-to-face with God. He had spent forty days and forty nights on the mountain, receiving God's revelation, and came down blazing radiant. His face was so bright that he had to put a veil over it to keep the Israelites from freaking out. Now, in verse 14, Paul says that in Christ "the veil is taken away."

There is another veil represented here, which was a curtain that hung in the temple, dividing the Most Holy Place from the Holy Place (Exod. 26:31). The High Priest would go behind the veil of the temple once a year on the Day of Atonement to offer a sacrifice for the people's sins. Only with this sacrifice could they enter the presence of God.

When Jesus died on the cross, God made one sacrifice for all time. Leave your bookmark in 2 Corinthians and turn to Matthew.

Read Matthew 27:51.

7. Here we see what happened to the veil when Christ died on the cross. Fill in the blank: The curtain of the temple was torn in two from _____ to _____.

So when Paul writes, "But whenever anyone turns to the Lord, the veil [over our hearts] is taken away," he means that through faith in Jesus's blood, shed for us on the cross, we can enter into that Most Holy Place; we can enter into the Presence of God, just as we are, right where we are. We can come to God, real and unmasked, with no separation between our hearts and his.

Now read 2 Corinthians 3:18 again.

8. What does this say God transforms us into when we come to him with unveiled hearts? Circle one:

   His daughter   His friend   His likeness

So God made us in his image; but then we sinned and shame covered our faces, and our hearts became hardened. When Jesus died and rose again, he demolished the separation between us and God. Now we can go face-to-face with him, on our knees and through the Word. As we allow him to remove the veil over our hearts, he transforms us to be more and more like him—renewing us in his image, the most beautiful image of all.

9. Use the space below to write about the image you reflect. Are you seeking to reflect the image of the world or Christ's image in the world?

10. Finally, share the state of your heart. Is it veiled or unveiled? Have you opened up your heart completely to God, so he can do his transformative work in you?

How might God want you to respond to what he's revealed to you today?

Close this day with prayer.

Lesson 10
Taking Off The Masks

Verse of the Day: "There is no fear in love. But perfect love drives out fear." 1 John 4:18

With all the focus on image in our world, it's no big mystery why our daughters and granddaughters are exponentially focused on their appearance. The media has tried and most often succeeded in branding the lie onto their brains: If something looks good on the outside, it must be good on the inside.

Because we are unveiling the nature of the father of lies here, let's take a quick look at where this lie originated.

The Lie

Read Genesis 2:16-17.

This is God's command regarding the tree of the knowledge of good and evil.

Read Genesis 3:4-6.

The serpent flat out lied about God; in fact, he called God a liar when he said, "You will not surely die." Of course, Eve fell for it.

1. What three things about the tree attracted Eve to eat from it?

   _____

   _____

   _____

Her appetite for beauty and power drove her to sin against God. Because the tree was "pleasing to the eye" and promised her wisdom, she bit the apple. Because it looked good, she thought it was good.

The Image of the World

Read Ezekiel 28:12-17.

This is a prophecy about the King of Tyre, who symbolizes Satan.

2. Write Ezekiel 28:12b here:

_____

_____

God made Satan a remarkably beautiful and wise angel, but it says here that Satan's heart became proud on account of his beauty and wisdom, thus corrupting it. So God threw him to the earth, making him a spectacle (28:17).

As "prince of this world," it's no surprise that Satan is doing the same thing to this generation of girls that he did to Eve—promising them that if something looks good, it is good. He tells them that if they listen to him, they will find the wisdom and fulfillment they long for.

So here we are in a world that worships not what is real, but what appears to be real: the image of what is good, instead of what truly is good. It's all about the outside appearance of things instead of the heart. The sad result of all this is that we can become like "white-washed tombs," looking good on the outside but rotting within. We get so adept at pasting on the smile that we get out of touch with our little-girl hearts, even when they are dying inside.

Burying the Truth

You have a choice in this section to either skim over the questions and apply them to someone you know, or to really look at yourself and identify the masks you wear. Naming my masks was the beginning of shedding them. When I let them tumble off, my little-girl heart became unveiled and that's when the transformation really began.

The following questions come from the story of Victoria (*Girl Perfect*, pp. 57-61). You may review it to refresh your memory if you like.

> **Highlighted Reading:** "I learned about the real girl beneath the image of Calvin Klein, behind the riding boots and starched white shirts. Underneath the image of that young girl looking innocently into the camera was a woman lost and running too… It was the world that she duped more than anyone. In ads, she was the image of self-assured beauty personified. Talk about an illusion. (p. 58).

3. How can something that looks so good be an illusion?

> **Highlighted Reading:** "Beneath the image, [Victoria] had no idea who she was or what her value could be. So I believe she wore a hard mask. She put on a tough façade as a way to protect herself from a world that had promised to make all her dreams come true but failed at every turn" (p. 60).

4. In what way (if any), do you relate to Victoria?

_____

_____

_____

_____

> **Highlighted Reading:** "In front of photographers, she was the epitome of confidence, wily seduction, and almost snobbish pride. But at home, she hated her reflection in the mirror, worried endlessly about being fat, smoked constantly, did drugs, and alternated between starving herself and bingeing. Victoria was as insecure and afraid in the world as I was" (p. 59).

5. How can pride and flaunting one's sexuality actually serve as a cover-up for fear and insecurity?

_____

_____

6. How often do you pretend to be OK when you are not? Put an X on the line below to represent your answer:

All The Time   Never
_____

7. What is your motivation when you do that?

_____

_____

_____

8. What is the mask, or image, you hide or have hidden behind?

9. What is the reason you wear masks to cover up how you feel? Be honest with yourself here so that you give the little girl inside of you a voice; she wants to speak.

> **Highlighted Reading:** "The mask kept her from being real, because if she was real, she would crumble. And she didn't have anyone in her life to pick up the pieces of her mess, so she fought to the death to hold on to the perfect image, even knowing it was an illusion" (p. 60).

10. Wearing a hard mask not only attempts to shield us from being hurt by the outside world, but also traps pain, fear, and memories within. What effect do you think this can have on a person?

_____
_____
_____

11. Do you have feelings that are trapped within? If so, what are they?

_____
_____
_____
_____
_____

12. How much do you put on a perfect image to shield how you really feel and to present a façade that is acceptable to others? Make an X on the line below to mark how heavily you depend on and prefer masks to honesty and authenticity. Be real here!

Rely on and Prefer an Image   Avoid Fakeness, Prefer
That Hides My True Feelings   and Choose Realness

_____

> **Highlighted Reading:** "After Paris, I had no idea how damaging an 'image' was—how making everything look pretty on the outside can often betray the little girl within. I also had no idea how far I would go to maintain the

> image. The truth is, I wanted to believe the image people saw in the pictures was real too. I was afraid that if I 'got real' about all I saw, felt, and experienced, it would ruin the image others had of my 'glamorous' life" (p. 61).

Fear is the greatest stumbling block to fulfillment and freedom. Not only was I afraid that "getting real" would ruin people's image of me, but I was also afraid of what I would do with the messed up details of my young adult years. If I told all of it, what then? Maybe people would reject me, but even worse, maybe I would reject myself. Maybe talking about sexual abuse, immorality, insecurity, drug use, self-hatred, and the rest would only prove to make it worse because I wouldn't know what to do with it or what it all meant. It seemed too big, too much, too messy, too complicated. It was safer to bury it.

13. What would stop you from getting real about the things that are buried in your heart? What do you fear about being honest about those things and actually giving them a voice?

Read 1 John 4:18.

14. Write 1 John 4:18 here:

15. If we are afraid, what does this verse say we are lacking?

_____

"Do not be afraid" is one of the most common statements God made to people in the Bible. He knew that when they were entering new territory, they would be afraid. Fear of getting real is natural. But God promises us that if we are real, he will transform us. As the veil over our hearts is removed and the soft flesh lies bare before him, he will gently go into those places, bind up what is broken, and fill in the gaps.

As we travel through the longings of our little-girl hearts, God will go with us into the darkest places, and he will take us through the darkness by hand into spacious places of light. His deliverance is his promise, and he never goes back on his promises.

Many of us from the younger generation are afraid that if we tell our mothers and grandmothers what we've been up to, where we've been, what we've seen, and what we long for, we will be seen as sinful and rejected as un-relatable. That's one of the main reasons why I've written this guide— to allow the younger ones freedom to be real and to be received like that. We older women had better receive the younger women as open, honest, and flawed if we intend to embrace a generation plagued with lies about where to fill their longings for perfect.

When you are real, you don't need to fear rejection from man because you are perfectly loved by God. Regardless of whatever sin or heartache lies within the deepest caverns of your heart that you think no one can see, you are adored by God beyond measure. That's why he sent his one and only Son to live and die, so brutally and humbly, for you—because he wanted you to know the desperate measure of his love for you.

Read Romans 8:28.

16. What does God promise to do for those who love him?

God intends to use your trials and triumphs for good. But if you don't ever get honest about the struggles you hide behind your mask, there is no room for him to use them for good. Because I open up about my life experience without shame, it is being used for good. I've given my life to God and asked him to use it for the benefit of his kingdom. My friend Patricia from Germany is doing the same thing by bravely sharing her story in this study. When she first wrote to me, her request was that her experience remain private. But over time, her heart became unveiled and she wanted to use the painful things in her life to shine a light to the hope we have in Christ.

When Eve was driven from the garden, she and her heirs became chained by the lie that everything had to look good on the outside for it to be received as good. And we know women like Tamar were told not to speak of their pain. But 2 Corinthians 3:17 says, "Where the Spirit of the Lord is, there is freedom." If you embrace that freedom with me to be unmasked, God will transform you into what he considers to be the perfect image—his image.

To See the Heart

We end the study today with a verse that unlocks our third truth. Read 1 Samuel 16:7b: "The Lord does not look at the things man looks at. Man looks at the outward appearance, but the Lord looks at the heart."

When the "woman who had led a sinful life" came to Jesus, she was trembling and afraid; in fact, she approached him from behind. She was a wreck. The religious people tried to condemn her, but Jesus received her. The longing of her little-girl heart—to be received without judgment—filled until it spilled over with gratitude.

Our third truth slays the lie, "If it looks good on the outside, it is good on the inside." Once again, the truth thunders from the voice of the Most High: "Man sees the outside, but I see the heart."

Truth #3

God says, "Man sees the outside, but I see the heart."

Give him your little-girl heart today. When you hand it to him, he receives it with the gentlest of hands.

> How might God want you to respond to what he's revealed to you today?
>
> _____
>
> _____
>
> _____

Girl Perfect Readings

Chapter 4—The Perfect Body:
Eating Disorders, Dissatisfaction, and the Battle for Control

Chapter 5—The Perfect Look:
Fashion, Pride and Real Beauty

Lessons

11: The Lord and the Body

12: The Longing and the Hunger

13: Perfection and the Body

14: Looking Good

15: Beautiful and Glorious

Lesson 11
The Lord and The Body

Read or reread *Girl Perfect*, Chapter 4, "The Perfect Body."

Verse of the Day: "You are not your own; you were bought at a price. Therefore honor God with your body." 1 Corinthians 6:19b-20

Lie #4
If you can control your body,
you are in control of your life.

The Longing:
To Be Beautiful

This lie tells us that our bodies are the sources of our strength, beauty, and value. Our bodies are things to be controlled. Certainly the message of our culture is that our longing for satisfaction and happiness can be filled by having an aesthetically beautiful body. If we look great, we are great, right?

This lie has an ugly twist. It is: Your body must be perfect to receive the praise of the world. Perfect, the world lies, is possible. Imperfect is ugly. So you should be shooting for perfect!

The Twist:
Your body must be perfect
to receive the praise of the world.

This generation of girls is crippled by poor body image more than any other. If the women of the church don't get a handle on this, our girls are in for worse trouble. As older women, it is our duty to teach them (Titus 2:4), so we must seek to understand their struggle. Why are the younger ones so confused about their bodies? Why are so many girls rejecting their gender? What are the lies they believe? And which longing in their hearts is driving them to such perfectionism, criticism, and self-loathing? The older women must take to heart the state of their daughters.

Many of us grew up watching our mothers detest their bodies, nip and tuck their faces and figures to death, and seek to fill their own longings for approval by the way they look. So many of us learned the lie from Mom.

The rest of us learned it from (on guard!) Satan himself. In the next lessons, we will unpack the lies about our bodies and replace them with truth that truly can set us free. Please pray for wisdom, discernment, and understanding as you go unveiled into the realm of your body and the bodies of the women and girls around you.

Body and Soul

One of the root causes of eating disorders and poor body image is the cultural idea that our bodies are separate from our selves. According to tradition, the body and soul are two different entities. The self, or the soul, in essence owns the body and has full rights over it. This concept has given birth to the right to choose. The pro-choice movement says, "It's my body, and I can do with it what I want." In other words, we own our bodies. They are our possessions.

Therefore, if we want to give our bodies away in sexual immorality, fine. If we want to abort children, fine. If we want to change our bodies with plastic surgery from top to bottom, fine! According to the lie—as promoted by the media—we own our bodies and can do with them what we please. Interesting, isn't it, that the media claim we can own something that we neither created nor bought!

STUDY GUIDE

But truth dispels lies. The truth is the body and soul are not separate, but intertwined. The inner self, or soul, is only able to express itself on earth through the body. Our bodies are the vehicles through which God projects his image. We are not separate from our bodies. Instead, through them, our spirits live, move, and affect the world around us.[1]

Using the parts of your body as forms of expression, write in the space below at least five ways you express your heart and soul on earth through your body, underlining the parts of your body as you go. For example, I might write: "The tips of my fingers tap the keyboard, forming words. My mind and heart work together to tell my hands what to write. My arms are used for hugging children, legs for taking walks, lungs for breathing air. My whole body coordinates to cook dinner for Shane, expressing love through service. I get down on my knees to seek wisdom from God."

1. Now it's your turn:

_____

_____

_____

_____

_____

_____

Read Luke 22:19-20.

2. When Jesus died on the cross for us, what did he offer in sacrifice? Circle your answer(s):

   His heart   His soul   His body   His earthly life

From your answer, would you conclude that there is a clear division between the body, heart, soul, and earthly life? Or would you conclude that they are intertwined? Circle the underlined word that best represents your conclusion.

Read Psalm 139:1-16.

3. Write down any feelings these verses invoke in you.

___

___

___

According to Psalm 139, he formed our bodies, so he knows them inside and out. If we choose Christ, his Spirit enters our bodies like light into a lantern. If we live according to that Spirit, God literally expresses himself through the vessels of our bodies. He gave each of us gifts, talents, and abilities that display the work of his Spirit on earth. As I travel around the country speaking to women and girls, I fully believe this. Through my body, God speaks through me (as long as I am depending on him for my words and not on myself). The same goes with my writing. I don't do any of this without asking God to work through me. Otherwise, it would just be me, instead of *him through me*. Without his Spirit breathing these words, they are powerless to change you.

4. How do you believe God expresses himself through you? What are some of your gifts that you think are ways God can or does manifest himself on earth through your body? Name at least three:

___

___

___

___

___

Read John 17:20-26, where Jesus prays for us.

Here Jesus prays that we would be brought to complete unity with one another and with him. He says that his hope is that he would be "in us" as God was "in him." In other words, Christ wants full union with us.

5. Is there any area of your life regarding your body that you are not allowing Christ "full union" with you? What is it and why are you holding that part of you back as your own territory to control?

___

___

___

Not Your Own

Read John 2:12-21.

6. How does Jesus feel about the temple of God? Circle all that apply:

   Complacent
   Passionate
   Consumed with emotion
   Showing personal interest
   Disinterested

7. What did Jesus call his body?

   ___

8. We know from 1 Corinthians 3:16 that the body is meant "for the Lord and the Lord for the body," and that "our bodies are members of Christ himself." What does that mean to you personally?

God is a lot more interested in the way we treat our bodies than we like to think. Satan, on the other hand, wants us to think God is disinterested in our bodies and that our bodies are our own possessions, to be manipulated by images we see in the media. Satan always sets us up to fail and leaves us feeling shamed. Sadly, he is so effective that he has turned many young women against their own bodies. It is up to us to claim the truth that sets us free.

Read 1 Corinthians 6:19.

9. Who made your body? Who owns your body? Who bought you at a price? Write his name in big letters here:

Now, I want you to get up from this study and walk away. Whether you nurture or abuse your body isn't in question. Just get up and move. Stretch. Walk. Dance. Raise your hands. Reach. Leap if you feel so inclined! Move slowly if that feels better. Your body is not separate from your soul. Whether its shape fits cultural standards is not the issue. You are made in the image of your Creator, and your body is his vessel for his Spirit on earth. It is not your own; it is made by him and for him. Experience and enjoy it.

10. When you come back, use the space below to journal about how this movement felt.

11. How could you better live out the truth that your body is not your own, but is instead "for the Lord"?

12. What impact would there be on your body if you actually treated it like it was his temple?

How might God want you to respond to what he's revealed to you today?

Close your time today in prayer.

Lesson 12
The Longing and The Hunger

Verse of the Day: "Paul looked directly at him [and] saw that he had faith to be healed…" Acts 14:9b

The lie we are exposing is that our bodies are things to be controlled and bent to our own demands for perfection. Every lie has a longing associated with it; that's how Satan gets in our heads and roots himself into our hearts. So what longing do we all have that leads us to believe the lie that our bodies must be controlled?

Certainly the overarching longing of the little-girl heart is to be loved with a perfect love. From that stems the rest—first, to be affirmed; second, to be accepted; third, to be received; and now fourth, to be beautiful. We all want to be beautiful, whether we admit it or not. We may each define beauty differently—some according to cultural ideals; some in opposition—but the longing is the same, projecting itself in varying lights.

The lies that I believed followed this progression:

I want to be loved.
To be loved, I must be beautiful.
Beautiful is thin.
Thin is controlled.
Controlled is acceptable.
Not controlled is not acceptable.
Not acceptable is not loved.

As often is the case, the lie begins with a truth: We want to be loved. But that love becomes conditional upon the state of the often uncontrollable reality of the flesh. The third link in the chain of lies, which says beautiful is thin, takes on many forms—all that define our worth. Some examples are: Beautiful is athletic. Beautiful is shapely, or, more specifically, beautiful is huge breasts, a tiny waist, flat stomach, tan skin—or beautiful is not being female at all. Here's one that plagued me: Beautiful is clear skin. This false thinking leads us to the sixth equation in the chain of lies, which deems us not acceptable because we can't control our bodies the way we wish we could. The final answer becomes unbearable; the lie stabs us right in the heart. Declaring our bodies uncontrollable, unbeautiful, and unlovable gouges the life right out of us.

Soul Hunger

We are awakening the longings of our hearts—in this case, to be beautiful—so we can identify the soul hunger that results from those longings not being satisfied. Of course, our method also is to reveal that which will no doubt fill the longing.

For some of us, our soul hunger has been fed all our lives; for others, it has been starved. I come to you as one whose soul is fed, full, and spilling over with truth; at one time, however, my heart was reduced by lies to a starved wasteland.

If you like, you can review *Girl Perfect*, pages 74-76, the story of Shellie, my bulimic roommate in Australia.

> **Highlighted Reading:** "…As she spoke, it felt as if her voice was coming from a far-off place, a small, young voice that called from beneath piles of rotten trash in Milan, Paris, New York — cries from a dumpster" (p. 75).

1. What do you think caused Shellie's soul hunger?

   _____

   _____

   _____

   _____

STUDY GUIDE

> **Highlighted Reading:** "The mirror was cropped, reflecting only my waist up. So I began to *look*, not in my eyes, but at my body…I felt the rows of sharp bones. My shoulders, which used to be broad, were now small and frail. Then I made myself look into my eyes—red, purple, hollow, deep, and black—there was no light left in them" (pp. 79-80).

2. What do you think caused my soul hunger?

   _____
   _____
   _____

Read Matthew 6:22 -23.

3. Fill in the blank: If your eyes are good, your whole body will be _____.

If the eyes are the windows of the soul, then soul hunger can be seen. In my work with young women, I look deeply into their eyes when we talk. I look beyond the mask. When meeting with a girl, I can usually see in her eyes if she is compromising her body in sexual impurity, popping pills, smoking weed, lying, and so on. On the surface, she may look great; her body may be sculpted, lean, and tan; she may be dressed well. But if her eyes are dark, how great is the darkness within her! I can recognize a girl like this because I was a girl like this. The spiritual and the physical are mysteriously intertwined, one expressing itself through the other.

Let's do an exercise. It's time for a stretching break anyway. Get up and go look at your eyes in the mirror. Look for emotion in your eyes. What do you see? Fear? Anxiety? Insecurity? Weariness? Hope? Confidence? Peace? Joy? If you are afraid to do this or feel like you can skip this part, then you had better get your rear end up and do it!

4. Describe what you saw:

   _____
   _____
   _____

5. Measure your soul hunger. Put an X on the line below to mark where your soul is when it comes to being spiritually fed:

   Nourished   Famished
   _____

6. Do you look into the eyes of the women and girls in your church/school/workplace? Circle one:

   Always   Sometimes   Rarely   Never

The older women need to learn to look into the eyes of the younger, and the younger need to look into the eyes of the older. Instead of doing this, we get caught up with externals—how we dress differently, how our bodies are different—and we miss being able to see the soul hunger in each other's eyes.

Read Acts 14:8-10.

7. How did Paul look at this man? At what do you think he was looking?

   _____
   _____
   _____

8. What state was the man's body in?

   _____

9. When Paul was speaking, this man was listening. Paul had the discernment to know that this cripple had faith. What kind of healing did Paul bring to the beggar? Circle one:

Spiritual healing
Physical healing
Both spiritual and physical healing

My friends, if Paul had focused on the man's body, he wouldn't have seen the man's soul hunger to be healed. The hunger was to be affirmed, accepted, received, and deemed beautiful enough and worthy enough of God's attention. Please don't miss how the healing began. It began with looking directly at the crippled man, in the eyes. It began with Paul's having the sensitivity to look directly at someone with whom he may have thought he had nothing in common. It began with believing he could connect on a faith level with anyone who wanted healing.

In the Eyes

I hear again and again that women of the older generation do not understand the teens and the twenties, and vice versa. Then when I go into a church to speak at a women's event, sometimes the leaders are surprised when I suggest to invite the teens. "The event is only for women," they say. "We have other events only for teens." Hello?! We can't figure out why the generations don't understand each other, but we don't ever get them together and give them a chance to go unmasked and look into one another's eyes. A few wise women in ministry are changing this, and it is making wonderful waves that I love to be a part of!

The Christians in Acts were not focused on the people's bodies, but on their souls. By focusing on the soul, they were able to minister in the body and in the spirit.

I lived in a world that wanted the perfect image, body, and look from me. Wherever I went, people focused on my body. That was my job. The photographers rarely looked me in the eyes; instead, they sized me up according to my flesh.

But there was one man, named Damien in the book, who looked me in the eyes upon our very first meeting, which was an interview for his magazine in Milan. He hired me for the magazine, and after the photo shoot, he took me to a delicious Italian dinner. Thus began our relationship. Looking for a father figure to protect and validate me, I was very drawn to him. We entered into a type of friendship and a business relationship in which I was the commodity. Because I refused him, the relationship never became physical, but it had tremendous negative impact on my self-image.

Before I knew Christ, I used to read tarot cards (which I now realize opens us up to the spirit of falsity). The night that I met Damien, I came home and fanned out the cards, asking the spirits to show me who he was. I pulled number 13 in the Major Arcana. The devil card. 666.

Damien expected perfection from me, and when I couldn't give it to him, he demeaned me. He fed me lie after lie after lie. My lovability was conditionally equated to my appearance and performance. The relationship left my little-girl heart crippled, deluded, and darkened by lies. No matter how hard I tried to resist his repetitive discussions of the "terrible suffering of life," that suffering became mine.

While I was writing *Girl Perfect*, I studied intensely what the Bible said about beauty, and that led me straight to the heart of the issue—the devil. So be praying for Christ's protection over your soul and the souls of the other women and girls doing this study while you proceed.

After Damien, the next three people who "looked directly at me" were Christians. They took the time to look past a stranger's body and into the windows of her soul. They gave me truth, truth, and more truth. They gave me Jesus, and that healed my body and my soul.

Thank God for them. As is the case with everyone from my travels I wrote about in the book, I have not seen or heard from them since. So it is my responsibility to tell you about them: it was real Christians who weren't afraid to look directly into the face of a lost and hurting girl who saved me... and that drew me to their church.

So...if you are seventy and don't understand why your granddaughter dresses the way she does, share your heart with her and see if she listens; look not at her clothing, but directly into her face. If you are seventeen and you don't understand why your mother is so overweight or overburdened, try to look beyond her image and into her soul; see if you can find some compassion there for what still needs to be healed in her. If you see a girl on the street who is down to a size 0, quit looking at her body! Look into her eyes! Maybe you have what she needs. She needs to listen to what you have to say; she needs healing. Above all, she needs to be received in her imperfect body and told she doesn't have to be perfect to be beautiful.

10. Have you ever longed for someone to look into your soul? What does that feel like?

___

11. Think of someone in your life whom you do not understand. How could looking into her eyes (not at her body/dress) change the way you see her? What might you see in the windows of her soul?

___

Pray for that person.

> How might God want you to respond to what he's revealed to you today?

Lesson 13
Perfection and The Body

Verse of the Day: "...the splendor of the heavenly bodies is one kind, and the splendor of the earthly bodies is another." 1 Corinthians 15:40b

Eating Disorders

I spoke at a church recently where I shared my testimony. Afterward many girls lined up to talk to me, most of them to confess their torment from eating disorders. The girls were famished to know someone comprehended their battle; they wanted to see face-to-face that healing was truly possible.

There they all were, crippled souls standing in line; they had listened to my message and had the faith to be healed. And at the end of the line, there I stood, looking directly into their eyes and offering hope.

> **Highlighted Reading:** "Whether we are bingeing and getting obese, starving and getting skeletal, or bingeing and purging in a roller-coaster ride of control, these are equally distant lines of the same triangle. Eating disorders are an outward reflection of an inner sickness. And the sickness stems from the heart at the center of it all: the longing. The longing to be validated, be paid attention to, to be loved and applauded and heaped with praise is so deep and so wide that it becomes a pit within us. And it is a pit that no amount of food, diet pills, deprivation, or purging can satisfy.
>
> "The scary thing is that we can die longing. The pit can swallow us alive. If we don't call for help, it *will* destroy us—body, soul, or both—because the quest for the

> perfect body has no final destination. Our bodies are ever changing, and they will never satisfy our demands for perfect. *Never*" (p. 81).

Check out these statistics:
1. At age thirteen, 53% of American girls are "unhappy with their bodies." This grows to 78% by the time girls reach seventeen.[1]
2. 6 out of 10 girls believe they would be "happier if they were thinner."[2]
3. 45.5% of teens report considering cosmetic surgery.[3]
4. Nearly 80% of young teenage girls report fears of becoming fat.[4]
5. 46% of 9-11 year-olds are "sometimes" or "very often" on diets, and 82% of their families are '"sometimes" or "very often" on diets.[5]
6. 70% of college women say they feel worse about their looks after reading women's magazines.[6]
7. While only 19% of teen girls are "overweight," 67% "think they need to lose weight."[7]
8. In girls aged 5-8 years, simply viewing a Barbie doll has been shown to reduce body esteem and increase a desire for thinness.[8]
9. Girls who frequently read glamour magazines related to weight loss are 6 times more likely to engage in extreme unhealthy weight control behaviors.[9]
10. Using social media for as little as 30 minutes a day can negatively change the way young women view their own body.[10]

Clearly, we have a serious "dis-ease" in this generation, so the people of God had better be educating themselves about and addressing it.

Bulimia: The Battle for Control

> **Highlighted Reading:** "For the bulimic, she hates her imperfections so much that she blames herself for them. She tries to control, control, control, and then she loses control and the shame eats her alive" (p. 82).

1. What is the relationship between bulimia and control?

2. What is the relationship between lack of control and shame?

> **Highlighted Reading:** "[Shellie] was *supposed* to have curves; she was supposed to look like a woman; she was not supposed to make herself sick to be a bag of bones. And she had to stop trying to be something she could never be—perfect" (p. 76).

3. What do you think the relationship is between eating disorders and perfection?

4. How would you help Shellie if she were your friend?

Anorexia: Thin Is Never Thin Enough

Let's be clear that these are grave physical and psychological conditions we are talking about here. The average human being can be of little help to people with eating disorders. Faith-based, trained counselors with extensive experience in these areas are the best. Please refer to www.girlperfectbook.com for a brief eating disorder screen, recommended reading, and counseling referral list for eating disorders.

Many people have asked how I healed from anorexia, so I'd like to answer that question. My experience with anorexia was a physical manifestation of a spiritual starvation. At the time, I was starving for unconditional love and acceptance and searching for a stamp of approval from the modeling industry.

Since I was never under a doctor's care, never diagnosed, and never given treatment, I am incredibly grateful that I was healed by the hand of the Healer. As I described in *Girl Perfect*, I fasted—not to lose weight, but instead to turn my life completely over to God. I begged and begged for healing, and he poured his love into my heart and filled my longing for approval. He taught me that how I looked in his eyes truly was all that mattered. As you will read in chapter 9, he removed the darkness from within me and bathed me in his light. After this experience, I was healed and free. The battle for control was over. I surrendered to him full control of my life, and over time I found a healthy weight and now have a good relationship with food. He had quenched my soul hunger.

My anorexia was directly tied to the modeling industry, to the pressure to be perfect, and to the fear that I would never be beautiful enough. Leaving the industry was a necessary step in my healing. The little girl inside of me couldn't have possibly flourished from that point on in a lifestyle that equated my value with my appearance.

Today it seems only natural that I would care for my body through regular exercise, stretching, and good nutrition. This body is not mine, but his. I want to care for it because through this body, God desires to project his love. For a freed daughter of God to neglect or abuse the temple of her body is in opposition to the will of the Spirit.

5. What do you think is the relationship between anorexia and the longing to be approved?

6. How do you think our quest for approval is tied to the longing to be beautiful?

> **Highlighted Reading:** "The ideal body, the world claims, is attainable, and it is OK that we spend the majority of our energies in search of it. But trying to make everything look perfect on the outside, for girls like Shellie and for girls like you and me, can be an exhausting, emotionally crippling, spiritually draining, and never-ending task" (p. 74).

7. Why is the quest for the perfect body so exhausting?

A Right Relationship with Our Bodies: Taking Care of Them

We won't spend much time in this context discussing how to take care of our bodies. Why? Because our culture is inundating us with diet plans, weight loss programs, gym memberships, classes, personal trainers, social media, and every other conceptual idea for us to lose weight and get fit. If we haven't figured out by now that eating healthfully and exercising regularly is the key to "being the best we can be in the skin that we are in," then, honestly, I'm at a loss. For those of us who are in good health (not battling diabetes or so on), taking care of our bodies is a fairly simple concept.

If it's a weakness in your life, however, please know this isn't coming from a place of judgment. I have been a size 2 to a size 14; sometimes I am great about working out regularly; sometimes I'm in a serious slump. We all have areas where we can improve.

But the bottom line is that eating lots of fruits and vegetables, drinking lots of water, watching our carbohydrate/protein/fat balance, and exercising two to five days a week is great for optimum health. My personal preference for exercise is to have a good balance between weight training, cardiovascular workouts, yoga, and Pilates. While weight training and cardiovascular workouts are great for muscle strength and burning calories, the quietness, stretching, and balance work of yoga and Pilates are phenomenal for the mind and the body.

8. How would you describe the care you give your body and what areas would you like to improve on?

_____

_____

_____

_____

The Truth About the Body

Read Genesis 2:4-7.

9. What did God make our bodies from?

　

Read Ecclesiastes 3:20, 12:7.

10. What will our bodies become after we die?

　

11. What does "dust to dust" mean?

　

　

My husband Shane had a dream once about what it's going to be like when Jesus comes back. He woke up totally amazed. Everything he dreamt matched up with Scripture. It was the kind of dream people who study the return of Jesus wish they could have, but God gave it to Shane, a normal guy. I love God. We don't have to be a theologian for him to show up and teach us about himself.

In the dream, there was absolutely no question what was going on when Jesus came back. "Everyone knew it was Christ," Shane said. There was an intense, blazing light, and in instantaneous flashes it pulled people into its tunnel, transforming them on the spot into their heavenly bodies and leaving their skin and clothes in heaps on the floor.

I asked him what the bodies looked like as they left the earth and entered timelessness. "They were intense," he said, "amazing, strong, as if they were made of muscle only. Perfect."

Read 1 Corinthians 15:35-54.

12. What body is the "seed"? (vv. 36-38,42-44) Circle one:

    The human body   The spiritual body

13. What is the relationship between the seed and the plant that grows from the seed?

    _____
    _____
    _____

14. What do you think it means that our bodies will be "raised in glory"? (v. 42)

    _____
    _____
    _____

15. What does this mean: "And just as we have borne the likeness of the earthly man, so shall we bear the likeness of the man from heaven." (1 Cor. 15:49)

    _____
    _____
    _____

16. What does this mean: "For the perishable must clothe itself with the imperishable, and the mortal with immortality." (v. 53)

    _____
    _____
    _____

STUDY GUIDE

Read Philippians 3:20-21.

17. What kind of bodies does this say we are going to have?

_____

Let's give that one a Hallelujah! Our bodies will be perfect and glorious! God knows just what we need in heaven.

Read Psalm 50:2.

18. Write Psalm 50:2 here:

_____

_____

He is the only one who is perfect in beauty and only he can fill our longing to be beautiful, by filling us with himself.

19. After studying this, what do you think about the idea that on earth—through working out, plastic surgery, Botox, and all the rest—we should strive for the perfect body?

_____

_____

Releasing Control

The longing to be beautiful is real; we all have it. But it is a lie that being beautiful has something to do with thinness or control. Can a girl with leukemia, cystic fibrosis, or a skin disease control her body? No. However, it is a deeply personal wound when we are rejected on account of our bodies because they are not separate from ourselves.

20. If you have experienced pain or rejection on account of your body, are warring with your body over disease or illness,

haven't cared for your body out of emotional distress, or are flat out worshipping your own image (your body) instead of the One who made it, then please take the space below to lay that at the Lord's feet and ask him to take the pain of that for you and replace your false hopes with truth. He wants nothing more than to heal you and set you free you from the lie.

_____

_____

_____

Our fourth truth replaces our fourth lie, which was, "If you can control your body, you are in control of your life." God's words of truth are: "Your body on earth will never be perfect, but as I fill it with my perfect beauty, you can release control to me. "

Truth #4
God says, "Your body on earth will
never be perfect, but as I fill it with my
perfect beauty, you can release control to me."

As his perfectly beautiful spirit takes up residence in our little-girl hearts, we can be free from the lie: control is not within our grasp, but in his all-powerful hands. Let go. Surrender control to him today in prayer.

How might God want you to respond to what he's revealed to you today?

_____

_____

_____

Lesson 14
Looking Good

Read or reread *Girl Perfect*, Chapter 5, "The Perfect Look."

Verse of the day: "'In the pride of your heart you say, "I am a god; I sit on the throne of a god in the heart of the seas." But you are a man and not a god...'" Ezekiel 28:2

Lie #5
If you've got it, flaunt it!

The Longing:
To Be Applauded

This lie is so prevalent in our world: "If you've got the body, if you've got the look, show it off! Strut your stuff, girlfriend! Get it!" Like our last lie, we see this one everywhere we look—TV shows, movies, magazines, commercials, Internet: it's in our faces. The media take very little responsibility for the exceedingly perverted lie that a woman's source of applause is her look.

As of this writing, research shows that:
- Twenty years ago, models weighed 8 percent less than the average woman. Today, they weigh 23 percent less, many falling into the anorexic weight range.[11]
- Seventy percent of women looking at fashion magazines report feeling depressed, guilty, and ashamed of their bodies within the first three minutes of flipping through the pages.[12]
- Half of teens say they want to lose weight because of magazine pictures.[13]
- In Great Britain, where it is reported that young women have the lowest self-esteem on earth, one quarter of sixteen-year-

olds are already considering plastic surgery.[14]
- One study showed that adolescent girls were more afraid of gaining weight than of nuclear war, developing cancer, or losing their parents.[15]

That last one is frightening. The lie has become so persuasive that their minds are becoming confused as to what really matters.

The first foreign translation for *Girl Perfect* was Korean. The publisher told me every girl in Korea needed to read this book. I was shocked, and then she told me why. In Asian countries, poor body image, depression, self-mutilation, and suicide are rising drastically among young women. Why? Part of the answer is that these precious girls will never be white, with blue eyes, double eyelids, and blonde hair. They will never look like Barbie, and that is what the world tells them is the perfect look. This is devastating for their self-image because they cannot change who God made them to be.

These facts bring such sadness to my heart. I was born in a body that ended up being six feet tall, with blonde hair and blue eyes. Does that somehow translate to me having greater value than the average girl in Korea? Does my frizzy, crazy hair make me of less value than someone with silky hair? Does my easily sun-burnt, easily broken-out, rapidly aging skin make me of less value than someone who doesn't wrinkle? Do I, with my faster metabolism and leaner build, have greater value than the missionary my ministry supports in the Middle East, who battles a thyroid condition, eats healthier than I do, works out five times as much as I do, but still has thicker, shorter legs and a wider build? Of course not! How horrible to even think it! These thoughts seem ludicrous and evil when written in black and white, don't they?

But the world keeps reinforcing these messages. Note the word forcing within the word reinforcing. The world repetitively brands the lie into the hearts of women and girls and causes them to believe that they need to change their bodies to keep up with the trends in the media in order to receive the applause their little-girl hearts so long for.

To Be Applauded

On the day I graduated from modeling school, I was walking across the stage to receive my trophy for Most Potential Model, and I looked out in the audience and saw my daddy standing up and applauding. At that moment, something registered inside of me that if I were a successful model I would earn his applause and the applause of the world at large. When I went to Milan in search of a spot on the runway, I was still that little girl in search of the same thing—the perfect look, the perfect affirmation, the success story, the whole bit. To be gut-wrenchingly real, I was after the applause.

But the applause of man didn't fill me. Whether your search for applause comes through your athletic ability, your intelligence, your mothering, your housekeeping, or your service to God, the longing is real for us all.

1. What does your need for applause look like?

2. Who do you need applause from the most?

3. When you don't get that need for applause filled, how do you feel?

Images of "Perfect" Beauty

> **Highlighted Reading:** "Somewhere along the line, however, we have distorted beauty to the point that it makes most of us feel *un*-beautiful. Looking at runway models or social media stars, the average girl—myself included—feels largely inadequate in comparison to them. None of us seem to measure up to that "perfect look." Not only do these women have what our world claims is a perfect body and a perfect look—they also have the perfect makeup, hair, clothes, walk, and confident air. Who can compete?
>
> "So beauty, as much as it is valued, becomes like mercury for most of us: the more we grasp for it, the more it seems to slip from our hands" (p. 95).

4. What is the perfect look the world claims we must have? Describe it here. (It doesn't have to be all physical, either.)

_____

_____

_____

5. How does the world's applause of outward beauty make you feel? How does it affect or not affect the way you see yourself?

_____

_____

_____

Most things that are worshipped and applauded on earth are not worshipped in heaven.

STUDY GUIDE

Prince of This World

Read John 14:28-31.

6. What does Jesus call the evil one?

   _____

   _____

7. As we remember from Genesis 3:1, the serpent is (circle one):

   Dull   Beautiful   Wise   Crafty

He is crafty, but if we wise up to his tricks, we find out that they are "same ole, same ole." Remember how he enticed Eve to question the truth of God for a lie? He deceived her little-girl heart, convincing her to believe that if it looked good, it was good.

Read Romans 1:21-23.

8. Here Paul describes people who knew God and thought they were wise for biting the apple (as Eve did), but they were actually fools. Why? For what did they exchange the glory of the immortal God? Circle the answer:

   Images that looked like God
   Images that looked like mortal men

Read Romans 1:25.

9. For what did they exchange the truth of God?

   _____

   _____

10. What did they worship and serve rather than the Creator?

11. How does our culture worship "images of man" rather than the image of God?

Read Romans 1:26-32.

12. How does this describe our culture?

When we exchange the worship of the image of God for the worship of the images of mortal men, boy, does that end up biting in the end—kind of like a snake bite! This shows us in black and white just how far the lie can take us away from the will of God. The lie is: "If you've got it, flaunt it, baby! Worship me! Worship this body! Bow down to me! Worship this look!"

I go to movies just like everyone else. I watch the Oscars on occasion. I've seen Project Runway, but I don't need to watch it, because I lived in that world. I know what it's like to be whipped up in a maelstrom of perfect looks that left me feeling empty.

So I don't close my ears or eyes to the world. I have an ear open to the voices of the world, but I keep my ear open to the voice of God even more. That's how I can separate evil from good, lies from truth.

Read Job 1:6-7.

13. Where and how does Satan say he spends his time?

Read 2 Corinthians 11:14.

14. How does Paul say Satan presents himself?

It's interesting that the Bible describes Satan as "masquerading," in other words, wearing masks that cover up what ugliness lies beneath, making himself out to be something he is not. As women who search for God, we have to reject the masquerade. We have to rebuke it and say it is not of God.

And, however deeply we feel the need to be applauded, we have to remember that only the worship of our Creator is beautiful; the worship of ourselves is depravity. If you don't believe that, or don't want to believe that because you allow your look to fulfill your longing to be applauded, just wait until you see what happens in the coming chapters of *Girl Perfect*; you will see where allowing my look to be worshipped left me: with my little-girl heart nearly buried in the depths of the sea.

Worshipping the Look

Read Ezekiel 28:1-2.

We are returning to this passage often in order really get to know the ways of the prince of the world. The more we understand the enemy of our souls, the more we are wise to his lies.

15. The primary sin of the King of Tyre was (circle one):

Lust   Greed   Pride

Tyre was a wealthy seaport through which vast monetary possessions flowed in and out. It was a very beautiful place on the coast, and in the eyes of the world, it had great riches. The King of Tyre symbolizes God's deepest loathing: pride. Satan will never be content with us worshipping our Creator. He wants us to worship him, a created thing. And the way the King of Tyre did this was by expecting himself to be worshipped on account of his wisdom, beauty, and wealth.

Read Ezekiel 28:4-10 and 17-19.

Satan flaunted his God-given gifts, believing they met his need to be applauded. So God hurled him to the earth, reducing him to eat ashes on the ground. Now he is slithering around trying to get our girls to put their pride in their "perfect look," their "wisdom," and their "wealth." These are the same things he tempted Eve with—beauty, knowledge, and fulfillment. Same ole trick, same ole trick.

It's time for some good news, isn't it?

The Good News

Listen now, deeply with your heart, to the voice of Jesus.

Read John 3:16-17.

16. What did Jesus come to do?

_____

_____

_____

Read John 12:27-33, the powerful words Jesus said when he was on his way to the cross.

17. By Jesus's death on the cross, who was driven out?

Read John 15:15.

At this leg of the journey, take this verse to heart. Jesus calls us friends. That's why he is revealing the whole picture to us—so that we can see him more clearly. My friend, I do not show you the ways of the devil to trouble you. I show you these things so that Christ may draw you to himself, that great tree of strength and power without which we are helpless in a lost and jaded world.

As it says in John 18:14, "It would be good if one man died for the people." In his death, the separation that sin causes between us and the glory of God was removed; the veil of the temple was torn in two. We can now see face-to-face.

18. Is there any way you are realizing that you have believed the devil's lies? If so, please put words to it here:

19. After what we have studied today, is there anything in your heart that you need to repent of?

Please close this day on your knees in prayer. Bow down to the Creator and repent of any way you have allowed your applause to come from the worship of yourself. Search your heart. Is there any pride, arrogance, or conceit there? If so, leave it at his feet and commit that you will worship him and him only!

Good things are to come, I promise you! Things that we can hardly imagine but are written in Scripture: pure wisdom, true riches, and endless beauty, unmatched.

> How might God want you to respond to what he's revealed to you today?

Lesson 15
Beautiful and Glorious

Verse of the Day: "Meanwhile we…[are] longing to be clothed with our heavenly dwelling." 2 Corinthians 5:2

In my day, the words *perfect*, *flawless*, and *beautiful* were being used more lavishly in advertising than ever before.

The word perfect was used to describe everything from lipstick to beer. It was everywhere we turned. Check out an old Victoria Secret's TV commercial for The Perfect One bra:

> I've finally found the One. The Perfect One. It shapes, smoothes, and supports, just like that! All in one bra. They say no one is perfect. Ha! You know what? You're looking at it. The Perfect One, from Victoria's Secret. I just love perfection.

I understand that this is marketing: "If you drink this, you'll feel good; if you eat this, you'll look good; if you drive this car, you'll be happy," and most of us know that's all a facade. But our girls are really suffering as a result of the lie that changing our bodies will stamp us "applauded and approved."

Today, we see overweight models, androgynous models, and women rejecting health, femininity, and their gender. There will always be trends driven by the media—so the question is, How will you make peace with your body, accept it like the temple of God, and care for it wisely? Or, will you cave to the trends and try to be someone you are not?

God's Girls

Read Isaiah 3:16-26.

1. What does it mean to be haughty? (v. 16)

2. Why did God take away the look of the women of Zion?

Read Isaiah 4:2.

3. What did he want to show them was truly beautiful and glorious?

So is God opposed to our purses and mirrors? Only if we are fools enough to think they are the source of our beauty. He took away the adornments of the women of Zion because they thought the adornment made them beautiful, instead of understanding that God within them was their source of security and power.

Read 1 Peter 3:3-6.

4. What do you think is the "unfading beauty of a gentle and quiet spirit, which is of great worth in God's sight"?

STUDY GUIDE

5. Who is "gentle and humble in heart"? (Matt. 11:29)

6. How can we be like the "holy women of the past"? (1 Pet. 3:5)

I always like to tell people that I'm not gentle and quiet by nature. I'm not! And how many of us are naturally humble? Not many. But I would rather humble myself than be humbled, as I've heard Beth Moore say. Like the women of Zion, I was humbled, so now I know that it is the glorious beauty of Christ within that gives me strength and power and that only Jesus deserves applause. Does that come naturally? No.

It comes from the process of understanding unfading beauty. The world's obsession with anti-aging techniques is symbolic for our quest for a beauty that won't fade; but the world can't change what fades away. Only God can.

When Moses descended from Mount Sinai with the Ten Commandments in hand, the radiance of his face was "fading away" (2 Cor. 3:13). Now 2 Corinthians 3:11 says, "And if what was fading away came with glory, how much greater is the glory of that which lasts!"

The beauty of Christ is unfading glory. Everything else pales in comparison. His is a beauty that lasts! That's why true women of God are radiant; they shine from the inside out. There are times when I don't feel radiant or feel as if I look radiant—especially when I've been up all night writing! But his glory fills me.

Read 2 Corinthians 3:18.

The Message version of this verse says that "our lives gradually becoming brighter and more beautiful as God enters our lives and we become like him."

7. Do you feel in your heart that you have an unfading beauty that is transforming you into being more and more beautiful from the inside out? Express in the space below how you feel. Keep in mind that I bared my heart in *Girl Perfect*. I felt so ugly at times. I know how that feels. So however you feel is OK. Open up the little girl inside of your heart here, and let her speak about how she feels about this beauty thing.

_____

_____

_____

_____

_____

_____

8. In the words of Jack London, from his book Martin Eden, "Beauty hurts you. It is an everlasting pain in you, a wound that does not heal, a knife of flame."17 Is beauty a "knife of flame" in you or is it "Christ in you, your hope of glory"? How so?

_____

_____

If you are turning to him with an unveiled heart, he is transforming you, even if the transformation is painful at times. And my dear sister, he is giving you the best makeover of all in this season, making you more and more like him, with ever-increasing glory.

The Perfect Look: Christ in Us, Our Hope of Glory

Read Isaiah 52:14 and 53:2-3.

9. List everything you learn here about Jesus's "look" on the outside.

_____

_____

_____

Read Isaiah 53:4-9.

10. List what you learn about Jesus's heart:

_____

_____

_____

Read Philippians 2:1-11.

11. What is beautiful to God?

_____

_____

_____

As God says in Isaiah 66:2b, "'This is the one I esteem: he who is humble and contrite in spirit, and trembles at my word." In one word, I'd have to say beauty is humility. Beauty is never allowing ourselves to be worshipped. In God's economy, where the first are last and the last are first, pride goes before the fall, and humility brings honor.

I have a friend whose son is a drummer for famous Christian artists. He gets tons of applause wherever he plays. She asked her son one day how he kept from becoming proud. He said, "God has given me a gift. It's not mine; it's his. I can't take the credit. So when they applaud, it's for him, not me."

We have to be guarded about the applause thing. In my case, God has given me a gift of communication through the written and spoken word. At the end of my talks, there is applause. As *Girl Perfect* reaches places on earth I never dreamed it would, I get wonderful letters. Positive feedback motivates all of us. The closet doors of my office are pinned full with letters and cards and photos of girls and women who have been touched by this ministry – and they mean so much to me! They motivate me to keep writing and speaking and pushing for the truth to be proclaimed, truth that will set the captives free (Isa. 49:9).

They—you!—are the driving factor for why I stay up all night writing and searching the Word for answers to the longings of our little-girl hearts. But I have to guard my heart from pride, which will ruin me. I have to keep myself in check so that I give the glory to the Perfect One who made it possible. And when I say, "The Perfect One," I'm not referring to my bra!

It's good to laugh. Proverbs 31:25 says that a woman of noble character is "clothed with strength and dignity; she can laugh at the days to come." Biblically, beauty comes in so many more forms that the flesh.

Romans 13:14 says we should "clothe ourselves with the Lord Jesus Christ." So if you are pretty, be humble about it. If you are smart, don't flaunt it. If you are wealthy, behave as if you are not. Don't take credit for whatever you are blessed with; instead, be like Jesus and show true humility to all men, always turning it back to the One who is to be praised.

This study would not be complete without a glimpse into the perfect outfit, the one we will be wearing in heaven.

Read Revelation 7:9-17.

12. What does it mean to have "washed [our] robes and made them white in the blood of the Lamb" (v. 14)?

Oh, how I long to be clothed with our heavenly dwelling (2 Cor. 5:2), where there will be no differences between us and where all applause goes to the Lamb at the center of the throne. But for now, we remain on earth.

13. If you clothed yourself with Christ during your days on earth, what do you think that outfit would look like on you?

My heart cries for you to know that you're longing to be beautiful can only be filled by allowing Christ's perfect beauty to shine from within you. Don't ever forget that to clothe yourself with Christ is the most brilliant outfit you can put on every day.

Our fifth truth, which replaces the prideful, from-the-heart-of-the-devil lie, "If you've got it, flaunt it!" comes directly from the voice of God: "You were created to reflect my beauty, not yours. Pride in external beauty is from the devil himself. The most beautiful look you can ever have is the heart of my Son."

Truth #5

God says, "You were created to reflect my beauty, not yours. Pride in external beauty is from the devil himself. The most beautiful look you can ever have is the heart of my Son."

How might God want you to respond to what he's revealed to you today?

Close this day with prayer.

Girl Perfect Readings

Chapter 6—The Perfect Dream:
Money and Success

Lessons

16: Money, Money, Money

17: Treasures in Heaven

18: The Threefold Dream
Part 1: The Spirit

19: The Threefold Dream
Part 2: The Crown

20: The Threefold Dream
Part 3: The Plan

Lesson 16
Money, Money, Money

Read or reread *Girl Perfect*, Chapter 6, "The Perfect Dream."

Verse of the Day: "You cannot be a slave of two masters…You cannot serve both God and money." Matthew 6:24 (GNT)

Lie #6
If you are successful and rich, you will be happy.

The Longing:
Joy

Take the Money and Run

Once again we are exposing a lie that we see everywhere we look—especially in the lives of the so-called stars of the world, which, by the way, are nine times out of ten in polar opposition to the definition of a star in God's eyes. The stars of the world give the impression that fame, wealth, and an abundance of possessions are a means to happiness. Then when those stars fall—through adultery, abuse, addiction, depression, divorce, and family collapse, the world is somehow shocked that those glamorous faces weren't as happy and fulfilled as they looked. Their masks of success were not at all reflections of real happiness, which is a much deeper concept: the joy of the heart.

I come to you as one who willingly admits that I wore a mask of success. I believed the lie. And the lie is so deceiving that most of the world believes it. It tells you that a godly dream for you—

happiness and fulfillment, which, when combined, create joy—can be found by achieving a worldly ideal.

One of the main reasons I pursued modeling was the money, no doubt. Modeling was my ticket to make money, which would buy me freedom to travel, which would then deliver me as happy and fulfilled, as the world had promised. People told me:

"Make the money, Jen."

"Take the money and run!"

"You can make thousands of dollars a day. Then you can take off, travel Europe, be free to do whatever you want to do."

"Just bite the bullet and make the money."

"Money will bring you freedom..."

"Do it! Make the money! You'd be crazy not to do it!"

These voices circled in my head. My mind became increasingly confused and despaired. I filled my journal with page after page of arguments between my body and spirit, which were constantly at war with one another.

Even when my soul cried out for freedom from the masks, I still kept pushing forward, waving my "plane ticket to freedom," saying it was going to take me to the destination I so desired! Why? Because the loudest voices in my head were the voices of the world, which promised me that money and success would fill the desires of my little-girl heart.

But my plane crashed and burned because I simply couldn't keep up the pace that it took to deny my soul its true longings. The longing to be happy and fulfilled got so big it began to swallow me alive. Sometimes we don't realize that we are trying to take a worldly avenue to fill a godly longing. The longing in this case, which we all share in our little-girl hearts, is for joy.

True Wealth

It's a shame that when I was going through all this, I didn't have an understanding of true prosperity. Since the Bible tells us that in Christ are hidden all the treasures of wisdom and knowledge, his Word will give us insight into what he defines as "The Perfect Dream" for all of us.

Read Proverbs 2:1-11 and 3:13-18.

1. To what do these verses liken insight and understanding? (v. 4)

2. What does Proverbs 3:14-15 say yields "better returns than gold" and is "more precious than rubies"?

3. What does Proverb 3:16 say is in the right hand of the one who finds wisdom and gains understanding? What is in her left hand?

4. In the space below, draw a picture of what Proverbs 3:16 says wisdom looks like. Make sure to label what is in her hands.

Leave your bookmark in Proverbs, then turn to Genesis.

Read Genesis 3:4-6.

5. What did the serpent convince her that listening to him would give her?

_____

_____

6. Turn back to Proverbs and read verses 2:1 and 2:6. Where does this say wisdom truly comes from?

_____

God's Word can be in polar opposition to the values upheld the world, can't it? Here we learn that instead of crying out for silver and gold, he wants us to cry out for wisdom—which will literally prolong our lives and bring us true riches and honor. We also learn

STUDY GUIDE

here that listening to Satan's lies does not bring wisdom, as he promises. Instead, wisdom is found in following God's commands.

Read Colossians 2:2-3.

7. What does this verse say are "full riches"? In whom does it say all the treasures are hidden?

8. Look back at your picture of wisdom. Who do you think that represents?

Read Ecclesiastes 2:4-11 and 17-26.

9. According to these verses, how does worldly wealth relate to happiness and fulfillment?

10. What do you think "chasing after the wind" means?

11. Ecclesiastes 2:23 says that when we are seeking an abundance of possessions, our work "is pain and grief;" even at night our minds "do not rest." Think about your own life. Does your

work bring you joy or does it cause you pain and grief?

12. What do you think God's will is for you in terms of your work?

13. What would true success in God's eyes look like for you?

As you complete this day of study, I want to thank you for being open and honest during this journey. Openness about things like money and what our hearts are really longing for—like happiness and fulfillment, or, better said, "joy"—can allow God an open door into our little-girl hearts. When we open up to him about what we're really looking for and any false ways we are trying to fill our longings, he can come in and shine his Word like a light.

Yet, when we invite him into our hearts, he may light up idolatry, which is the worship and idolization of other things before God. As Jesus turned over the tables of the moneychangers in the temple, he may do the same in us. And I hope he does! Because when he turned over the tables of the moneychangers, he was clearing the temple of sin. Zeal for his father's house consumed him (John 2:17).

He has that same zeal for us—because we are his father's house. The first verse that ever gripped my heart and made me stop in my tracks was, "You cannot be a slave of two masters...You cannot serve both God and money" (Matt. 6:24, gnt). I read that verse at my kitchen table in Munich the very first time I read the Bible in my life. It convicted my lifestyle and everything I was looking for. But it also gave me a choice: Serve that which will turn out to be meaningless in the end, or serve the one who crowns us with "everlasting joy" (Isa. 35:10). That choice is yours too.

How might God want you to respond to what he's revealed to you today?

_____

_____

_____

Lesson 17
Treasures in Heaven

Verse of the Day: "For where your treasure is, there your heart will be also." Matthew 6:21

The issues we have with money are similar to the issues we have with beauty. The world tells us, "If you've got it, flaunt it! The more the better! Money will bring happiness and fulfillment. Go after it! Seek money, not wisdom." Yet God's Word teaches that if we seek wisdom, we find true riches. Once again, God's economy is upside down: the first are last; the last, first!

Continuing to take a close look at the nature of Satan helps us identify the lies that bind us.

Read Ezekiel 28:4-5.

1. In this section, what was the source of the King of Tyre's pride?

   _____

Read Ezekiel 28:13.

2. What do you think all these costly stones represented?

   _____
   _____
   _____

Read Revelation 21:9-14 and 18-21, giving special attention to verses 19-21, the list of stones.

Here we see a picture of the New Jerusalem, God's Holy City, God's future home for his people. When the church, the bride of

Christ, unites with him in heaven, it will be beautiful and glorious. As verse 11 says, "It [will shine] with the glory of God, and its brilliance [will be] like that of a very precious jewel…"

3. With what will the foundations of the city be built? (vv. 19-20)

_____

_____

4. Describe the gates and the great street of the city. (v.21)

_____

_____

_____

Clearly, this is a place of incredible wealth!

Leave a bookmark in Revelation, as we will come back to it.

Read John 14:1-3.

5. What kind of place is Jesus preparing for us?

_____

_____

_____

Read Revelation 21:22-27.

6. Now this is a place we want to be! Try to describe it:

_____

_____

_____

STUDY GUIDE

Read Isaiah 60:1-5, the Glory of Zion.

7. When all the wealth is brought to the throne, what will our hearts swell and throb with?

_____

Read Isaiah 60:11.

8. What will men do with the wealth of the nations at the wedding of the Lamb?

_____

_____

Read Isaiah 60:17-21.

9. What will God give us on that final day? (v. 17)

_____

10. What will we possess forever? (v. 21)

_____

What greater joy could we possess but to know that all the jewels, all the wealth, and all the riches on earth came from him and some day we will in triumphant procession bring them to him on streets paved with gold? What greater joy could we possibly have to know we will possess eternal treasures and bathe in eternal light, forever?

Read Matthew 6:19-21.

11. With what Jesus knew about heaven, it must have been almost maddening for him to see people on earth holding tightly to their possessions. What is he telling us here?

_____

12. What does this mean, "For where your treasure is, there your heart will be also"? (v. 21)

Read Matthew 6:25-34.

13. What is Jesus saying about worrying over worldly things?

14. If we seek first his kingdom, what does he say he will do for us?

From Ezekiel 28:14, we learn that Lucifer was a "guardian cherub," a higher-ranking created spiritual being who possibly guarded or protected the throne of God. The stones that adorned him were the very same stones listed in Revelation as paving the foundation of the new Jerusalem; and they were the same stones upon which he walked in Eden.

But even with his amazing wealth and high standing, Satan traded truth for a lie. He wanted to be worshipped; he was deceitful and shameful, so he will not enter the heavenly gates by which he once stood. Instead, God reduced him as far as one can be reduced; from the throne room of God to eating dust, slithering on his belly as a loathsome snake. Mr. Lucifer must not be very happy about that.

15. The King of Tyre was "rich." He wore jewel-spangled robes; he had it all. But did he really? Think about your answer to this question.

Selling Your Soul

Read Mark 8:36-37.

16. Write Mark 8:36-37 here:

Read Matthew 27:1-5.

It's pretty safe to say that Judas sold his soul for thirty shekels of silver. The end result was dreadful. He hanged himself. Selling his soul ended his life on earth and resulted in eternal darkness and death. Was it worth it? I think not.

Read Acts 5:1-10.

17. What is the result of selling our souls to retain money on earth?

No Price Tag

You can't put a price tag on what we have in heaven. It can't be bought; it can't be sold. Instead, without money or price, you were bought with the blood of the Lamb, so that he could show you his house one day.

As Ecclesiastes 7:12 says, "Wisdom is a shelter as money is a shelter, but the advantage of knowledge is this: that wisdom preserves the life of its possessor." The longing we have for joy is found by possessing true riches. Oh, I can hardly wait; I can hardly wait!

> How might God want you to respond to what he's revealed to you today?

Lesson 18
The Threefold Dream
Part 1: The Spirit

Verse of the Day: "And I will ask the Father, and he will give you another Counselor to be with you forever – the Spirit of truth." John 14:16-17a

Hello, my friend. I hope you are drawn to this journey as much as I am. Make sure you check your masks at the door. There's no use for them here! In these next few days, God wants an open door to your heart so his light can stream in. He wants utter transparency, no facades, no pretending.

> **Highlighted Reading:** "God's perfect dream for you is threefold. First, it is that you know his love and therefore experience the peace and security of walking with him. Second, it is that he heals your broken heart, and brings beauty from the ashes of your life. Third, it is that you discover his plan and purpose for you" (p. 128).

For the next three lessons, we are going to talk about God's "Perfect Dream" for you, and how discovering and living that dream produces real, lasting joy.

When I first came to Milan, I used to run in the neighborhoods surrounding my apartment. There seemed to be churches on every corner in that city. As I whipped around the bend of my neighborhood in the mornings, my running shoes propelling me forward, I used to pass a church that had a revolving door. Around the corner from the church was a cappuccino stand, where people lined up for their morning espresso doppio and yummy pastry. As I headed toward the train tracks across the street, I would turn back to see the people all bundled up, their breath steaming in the crisp morning air, going in and coming out of the church in a steady flow. Then they would get their coffee, board their train, and go on to work.

One day curiosity got the best of me, and I went through the revolving door, running clothes and all. Inside, a hushed whisper filled the cavernous space; the only sound was the muffle of feet and muted, under-the-breath prayer. Straight ahead, stretched before me was a long, worn hardwood aisle that led to a massive cross up front. To the left of the entrance was an alcove where people were lighting little red tea candles, kneeling in prayer, and signing the crucifix over their chests: fingers pointing quickly—head, heart, left, right—the cross.

I didn't know what it meant. I watched and left.

A week or two later, my tennis shoes skidded to a stop on the sidewalk once again and led me through the "in" side of the revolving door. I wanted to light a candle the way the old ladies did in the morning. It seemed like such a sweet way to begin the day. Thinking of my many castings ahead, including the Armani ones, I lit a candle, bowed my and prayed quietly for my success in Milan.

I didn't know whether or not there was a real God, one who heard me. But that prayer was answered. From what my agencies saw, I was very successful over there, making all that money, appearing in the magazines, doing the runway, the covers.

It was just a few months later that felt such a vast longing for love that it was like someone took a stick and hit me on the back the knees with the loneliness, knocking me down to the hardwood floors of my own apartment. Success didn't mean happiness at all, and I wept for lack of fulfillment. I finally prayed, "Thank you for my success, God ... but all the money and magazines and clothes don't mean anything to me without love. Please, if you hear me, send me someone to love. I beg you; that's all I need" (p. 113).

No matter what dreams we are chasing, someone to love is what we all want, isn't it? Someone to make us happy, someone to laugh with, someone to weather the storms of life by our side. It gives me great joy to share with you that prayer's first answer, which was my beloved *Bosquo*, that rumpled little dog I adopted in Italy.

The Perfect Companion

> **Highlighted Reading:** "The perfect dream for all of us is that... there will be *someone* who will stick by our side... someone who won't leave us for any reason or excuse. We want someone whose love is not based on our performance. We want to know that if everything unravels, we will have someone who knows our hurts and is willing to tend our wounds when invited" (pp. 126-127).

1. Have you ever had a companion like this—an animal or a special friend—who stuck by you the way Bosquo was loyal to me? If so, name that companion here and the impact he or she has had on your life.

Some of us call these kinds of companions "God with skin on." If we ask God for the kind of love that will truly heal us, it is his joy to give that to us, but it may come in unexpected forms!

Read Luke 11:11-13.

2. What does this verse call the Holy Spirit? Select one:

   A good leader   A good friend   A good gift

Read John 14:16-18.

3. How did Jesus describe the Holy Spirit?

   _____

4. Where does this verse say the Spirit will live?

   _____

Read John 17:26.

5. Who did Jesus say will be in us?

   _____

   _____

   _____

> **Highlighted Reading:** "In Christ, there *is* a 'happily ever after.' In Jesus, God offers you the perfect companion, the One who will not leave your side and will love you through every situation and circumstance, good and bad.
>
> The Holy Spirit, who is given to all who believe, is forever faithful, kind, and full of grace. As you walk through life, God's Spirit within you gives you direction and discernment. And as Kim said, God's Spirit protects you; he offers security. The Spirit of God does not always prevent you from going through trials, but he walks with you through them. Finally, his Spirit is a deposit, guaranteeing what is to come: eternal perfection—heaven—when you get to be with God all the time..." (p. 129).

"God has said, 'Never will I leave you; never will I forsake you'"(Heb. 13:5b).The Holy Spirit within us is the love of God "poured out [in] our hearts" and it never leaves us alone, because it dwells within (Rom. 5:5).

The enemy will try to whisper in our ears that the companionship of God is not enough, as he did to Eve and to Jesus. I'll never forget Damien looking me square in the eye, his pupils as small as the most potent espresso bean, saying, "When is the last time you have been with a man? A man is what you need, but instead you have taken this dog from the Bosquo [the woods]. How terrible! What you really need is a man, but a man will leave you, so instead you have stolen this poor dog from the Bosquo, and taken her to this disgusting city. How selfish! You should take her back. Or, if you bring her to America, you take her to *la montana* and let her go. She will walk away from you and never even turn her head to look back. She will forget all about you!"

Are we getting to the point now where we can recognize the voice of the accuser? Damien's words remind me of Judas, pointing the finger at Mary of Bethany as she poured her heart out to Jesus, saying, "Look at this woman! What a fool! What a waste! Of course, Jesus rebuked him, saying, "Why are you bothering her? She has done a beautiful thing…" (Mark 14:6).

The love of God is never wasted on us, and it is always beautiful. I did move to the mountains of America, by the way, and although Bosquo wandered unleashed there many times, she never abandoned me. She proved to be a true companion.

The Holy Spirit is the Spirit of Truth that will guide us into all truth (John 16:13). The spirit of the world, however, is the spirit of falsehood. The world's companionship turns out to be counterfeit, giving the appearance of comfort and love, but in fact it is useless for producing the joy we so desire.

Because we all long to be loved, we must be careful that this longing does not lead us into accepting a counterfeit companion into our hearts in hopes that he or she or it can bring us the joy that only God can give.

The Counterfeit Companion

In our loneliness and fear of being alone, we can become so weak. It confounds me how many women and girls tolerate abuse in their relationships. Statistics say about one in five high school girls

Over half of students report dating violence among their peers.[2] Women account for 85% of intimate partner violence, and women ages 20-24 are at the greatest risk of it, regardless of race or economic status.[3]

In search of companionship, we can so easily be led to accept less than our little-girl hearts deserve.

When I was in Milan, you will recall that I wanted desperately to run away and clear my head, and so I decided to go to Venice. As you know, that weekend Damien sent his son with me to "protect" me, which turned out to be fraud. There his son took advantage of my weakness resulting from having my deepest longings so unfulfilled. Having been a fighter and a protector of myself all my life, I know now that I was in a soul-less state not to defend myself against the invasion of this man into my life and heart.

Just to give you an idea of the state of his soul, he had a tattoo of a venomous serpent on the back of his neck.

Not surprisingly, that snake came knocking at my door again in Milan. Just when Damien cast me aside, refusing me his companionship, and I suddenly had no one to "have dinner with," there came his son knocking, offering to cook me dinner. And just like Eve, I entertained his lies.

In want of companionship, we can be so stupid. When we tolerate a counterfeit companion in cases like these, we have to take ownership of the fact that we opened the door to it. We cannot just blame the serpent; we are to blame as well.

It's even more indicative of sickness when as Christians we allow a counterfeit companion to enter our hearts in hopes of getting our longings filled. Recently I developed a friendship with a beautiful, intelligent Christian woman who was also a single mother. Very impressed by her, I encouraged her to take a leadership position in ministry. But God soon revealed that she was allowing herself to be physically abused. In hopes that a man would offer her the hope and future she so desired, she was allowing her little-girl heart to be trashed.

When I meet girls and women who know the Lord yet tolerate abuse or accept a counterfeit companion, I see that as so contradictory to the purpose Christ died for. The enemy comes to destroy our hearts; Christ comes to bind them up. When we believe love can somehow be rooted in abuse, we are terribly wrong. And, we are missing out on the life-affirming love our Savior desperately wants for us.

No matter where we've been or what we've done, the moment we put our faith in Christ, we are crowned his daughters. Our bodies are his temples and our hearts are to be vehemently guarded as the wellspring of our lives (Prov. 4:23).

The longings of our hearts are deep and tumultuous waters, and we all long for the "dream." But we have to be so very careful. Ladies, if it moves like a serpent, talks like a serpent, lies like a serpent, and seduces like a serpent, let me help you out: it is a serpent—no matter how good that "angel of light" makes things look on the outside. Remember, his trick is the masquerade. He makes things look good to cover up ugliness beneath the surface.

Just as in the garden, the snake promises that things will be better if we listen to him. He allures us with things that "look good, taste good, feel good," telling us they are good. But when we bite into his lies, he leaves us feeling ashamed.

6. Have you ever been with a counterfeit companion? Circle one:

   Yes   No

7. Have you ever been with someone who has abused you? Circle one:

   Yes   No

8. If your answer to either of the above questions is yes, please use the space below to describe what motivated you to do so and how the relationship made you feel:

   _____

   _____

   _____

   _____

   _____

   _____

For those of you who have willingly allowed yourself to be with a counterfeit companion or an abuser—or have a loved one who is—I know this is hard! But fight with me! Press on!

We are going to learn something essential here. Open your Bible now; take out your sword. On guard, ye faithless serpent! God is bigger than you and is going to crush you (Rom. 16:20)!

Read Genesis 3:1-23 carefully.

9. Check the emotions that the couple experience:

STUDY GUIDE

- ☐ Feeling afraid
- ☐ Feeling afflicted or wounded
- ☐ Feeling ashamed
- ☐ Feeling banished, cast out, thrown out
- ☐ Casting blame
- ☐ Feeling cursed (injured or lowered to a menial position)
- ☐ Feeling confused
- ☐ Feelings of enmity (hostility or hatred)
- ☐ Feeling deceived
- ☐ Feeling guilty
- ☐ Feeling hurt
- ☐ Feeling lost or separated from God
- ☐ Feeling tricked or lied to
- ☐ Experiencing pain and turmoil
- ☐ Experiencing shame associated with nakedness

I hope you checked them all. If the counterfeit one wiles his way into your heart or a loved one's heart, these same feelings will apply.

1 Thessalonians 5:21 says we are to "test everything [and] hold onto the good." 1 John 4:1 says we must "test the spirits to see if they are from God." Therefore we must test to see if we are relying on a counterfeit companion or a true companion for our joy.

The Litmus Test

Read Matthew 7:15-20.

10. How do we recognize falseness? (v. 16)

    By its _____.

Read Galatians 5:19-26.

11. Some translations call the "acts of the sinful nature" the "works of the flesh." Under the headings below, list the works of the flesh and the fruit of the Spirit.

Works of the Flesh	Fruit of the Spirit
_____	_____
_____	_____
_____	_____
_____	_____

All trees are recognized by their fruit; both true and counterfeit companions apply. Relationships with people as well as with things need to be tested by their fruit. If their companionship brings you joy, serenity, loyalty, compassion, and the like, you know it's good, and those forms of it should be nurtured. If it brings you division, heartache, shame, banishment, deceit, and the like, you know it's bad.

John 15:2 says that God "cuts off every branch" that "bears no fruit, while every branch that does bear fruit he prunes so that it will be even more fruitful."

First, we must identify the fraud for what it is. Then, if you or a loved one is in a relationship with an abuser (the counterfeit companion may come in the form of a man, a drug, a love of money, or a false way of finding real joy), then that relationship must be cut off. If you have to get up and run from it, then run. That's what I did: I ran far and fast. And when I did that, I ended up running right into the arms of my true Father. He became my True Companion and later gave me a healthy companion. God is good, all the time.

Let's pause for a moment to pray:

> Father, thank you that you unveil the lies of the enemy for us so that we can learn to recognize them. Thank you that it was your will for your Son to suffer shame for us so that we do not have to suffer shame. Thank you for the Holy

Spirit within us that gives us wisdom, knowledge, and discernment. Help us, Lord, to be open to your pruning. Sometimes the pruning hurts, God, but we know it is for our benefit. Direct us, Lord, into the fruitful, abundant life you want to give us through your Son. In Jesus's name, amen.

Finally, read John 16:13.

12. Why is the Holy Spirit the perfect companion?

13. How does he bring us peace and security?

The first part of the threefold dream God has for you is that you know his love and experience the peace and security of walking with him. If you allow the Holy Spirit to be your true companion and faithful guide, if you listen to his voice and follow his direction—when it hurts and when it doesn't — you can't go wrong.

How might God want you to respond to what he's revealed to you today?

Lesson 19
The Threefold Dream
Part 2: The Crown

Verse of the Day: "Blessings crown the head of the righteous…" Proverbs 10:6a

Whether our counterfeit companions are made of flesh and blood or are the things of this world, we are learning that they have no hope of filling our longings. The longing for joy is so real that we might look in all the world to find it. The world tells us happiness and fulfillment come from worldly success, but God's economy is upside down; with him, joy comes from unexpected places.

The second part of the threefold dream God has for you is that he desires to heal your broken heart and bring beauty from the ashes of your life. This is the subject of today's study.

A Heart Healed

> **Highlighted Reading:** "God's perfect dream for you is simple but profound. According to Isaiah 61:1, Christ came to bind up your broken heart" (p. 129).

Read Isaiah 61:1-3.

1. What did Christ come to do?

   Preach the _____ to the poor.

   Bind up the _____.

   Proclaim _____ for the _____.

   Release from _____ for the _____.

   Proclaim the year of _____ and the day of

_____ of our God.

To _____ all who mourn.

And _____ for those who grieve.

To bestow on them a crown of _____.

The oil of _____ instead of mourning,

And a garment of _____ instead of a spirit of _____.

No matter how many times I read this, I am amazed, humbled, and overwhelmed by it. God has done all of this for me, and his dream is to do all of this for you and for every person on earth, if we would just open our hearts to him.

> **Highlighted Reading:** "It has been extraordinarily painful for me to open up the deep recesses of my heart and let the truth pour out in this book. But as I have done so, Christ has come in and healed the most painful of places within me: the loss of my innocence, the stolen sense of security and worth, the feeling that I was only "flesh," that I was never good enough, and that the perfect dream really *wasn't*, which caused misunderstandings between my family, whom I love so much, and me. Some wounds have been slow to mend" (p. 129).

2. Do you have any wounds that have been slow to mend? What are they?

_____

_____

_____

_____

_____

The good news is that you may not be called, as I was, to put them in print for all to see! But you are called to give your heart to him. The Holy Spirit pours perfect love into our hearts, but he will only do that if we allow him. If we keep the deepest corridors and recesses shut to him, he will not force his way in, no matter how much the living water of his Spirit desires to flush out those places of darkness and cleanse them.

> **Highlighted Reading:** "That trip to Venice took the wind out of my sails completely...It was the final nail in the coffin of the little girl who once was. So this was just another mask I had to wear—the mask that says, 'Nothing in me hurts. It's all good. All smiles'" (p. 114).

3. Do you have anything in your past that buried the little girl that once was? If so, name it here:

> **Highlighted Reading:** "I daydreamed of crying from the hurt and it not mattering that my eyes got red and swollen from the honesty of it all. I daydreamed of *freedom*, childhood freedom...Beneath the masquerade, I wanted a better fairy tale, the one where I was known, seen, and loved for who I was underneath all the layers..." (p. 115).

4. Do you know what this feels like? If so, put words to it.

_____

_____

_____

_____

> **Highlighted Reading:** "We don't want to be forgotten. We don't want to be cast aside. We don't want to be *unwanted*" (p. 127).

5. Have you ever felt cast aside, forgotten, or unwanted? If so, describe what that felt like for your little-girl heart:

_____

_____

_____

The Book of Ezekiel describes such a soul, in the persona of a baby girl who is rejected and despised.

Read Ezekiel 16:4-8.

The imagery of these verses describes Jerusalem, often referred to through the Word as a woman. Because you are a woman, we can apply these words to the way that God sees you. In verses 4-5, the Lord describes a child (let's think of her as our little-girl hearts). This little girl has been thrown out and abandoned. She is alone, and kicking about in her blood and shame. But God says, "Then I passed by and saw you...and said to you, 'Live!'...when I looked at you and saw that you were old enough for love, I spread the corner of my garment over you and covered your nakedness. I gave you my solemn oath and entered into a covenant with you, declares the Sovereign Lord, and you became mine"(16:6-8).

STUDY GUIDE

Our deepest wounds most often come from those who are closest to our hearts. In this case, the little girl didn't have a mother and father who were protecting her. But when she was alone and afraid, God saw her and called her, "Mine"; he made her his own.

Keeping a bookmark in this passage of Ezekiel, turn to Psalms.

Read Psalm 27:10.

6. Write Psalm 27:10 here:

_____

_____

_____

For some of us, the ultimate in rejection comes not from our parents but from our spouses, which can be equally painful.

7. Read the following verses and write in the space below them how God can act as mother, father, and even spouse to us when we feel rejected or abandoned:

Isaiah 49:15

_____

Isaiah 54:5-6

_____

Isaiah 63:16

_____

8. In a world that emphasizes performance, what is it like for our little-girl hearts when someone loves us just because they love us, not because we have met any expectations for them?

_____

_____

Whenever we are discarded or thrown out, God stands up and sees it. He rescues us and says to us, "Live! Become mine!" And then, when we are ready, he lavishes us with his love, restores us, and gives us a beauty that lasts.

Turn back now to Ezekiel and read what he does with the abandoned and discarded. Let every word soak into your heart like a rushing stream.

Read Ezekiel 16:9-14.

9. What do you think it means when he says, "I bathed you with water and washed the blood from you and put ointments on you"? (v. 9)

_____

_____

_____

10. What do you think the adornments he dresses the daughter with symbolize?

_____

_____

11. Fill in the blank:

"I put a...beautiful _____ on your head...you became very _____ ... because the splendor I had given you made your beauty _____." (Ezek. 16:12-14)

12. What meaning does this story have for you?

No matter what the world does to us, we are received by God. The desire of God's heart is to restore us from whatever ashes the enemy has tried to put us in and crown us as daughters of the King.

The Crown

The enemy wants to keep us wallowing in our ashes because that is where he is; but God wants the opposite; he wants us to "rise up" in "garments of splendor" (Isa. 52:1-2). If some of your "tickets to freedom" have led you on plane rides that crashed and burned, if some of your dreams seem to have been reduced to dust, Christ came to raise you from them and restore the value for which he created you in the first place. He came to crown you; don't you ever think any different.

Read John 19:1-16.

13. What kind of crown did Jesus wear so that we could wear a crown of beauty?

Read Proverbs 10:6.

14. We know that faith is credited to us as righteousness. What does he crown the righteous with?

Read Isaiah 51:11.

15. What does this verse say will crown our heads when we enter Zion?

___

I'd like to share a poem by Frank J. Zamboni with you that hangs in a gold frame in my office; the words are hand-stitched on linen cloth, trimmed in old lace. My mother-in-love, Linda, a wise and beautiful soul, gave it to me many moons ago.

> I said a prayer for you today
> And know God must have heard.
> I felt the answer in my heart
> Although he spoke no word.
>
> I didn't ask for wealth or fame
> I knew you wouldn't mind.
> I asked him to send treasures
> Of a far more lasting kind.
>
> I asked him to be near you
> At the start of each new day;
> To grant you health and blessings
> And friends to share your way!
>
> I asked for happiness for you
> In all things great and small.
> But it was for His loving care
> I prayed the most of all![4]

That's my prayer for you today: that you would find true treasures. Wealth and fame on earth turn out to be less than they are cracked up to be. Happiness. Protection. Health. Blessings. Friends. Family. These are what count. And, of course, these are what God wants for us. Consider the words of Christopher McCandless, whose journey was the subject of the movie *Into the Wild*. He "ran away from it all" in search of "freedom" and ended up dying from lack of community. Written next to the place where he died were his words: "Happiness is only real if shared."[5]

I am going to count my blessings now and then ask you to count yours.

> *In the dark of the early morning, I sit with a candle lit, soft music playing in the background. The Presence of God is here with me. Despite the trials we are facing, there is joy in my soul today. My white Labrador retriever is curled up at my feet. I have the Word before me that has more verses on joy than I could begin to unravel. But what I can pinpoint today is this: my blessings. Our son Zach sleeps soundly in his bed upstairs, his little heart resting from how hard and fast he played yesterday. Olivia is nestled in the strong arms of her daddy this morning, having woken from a leg cramp in the night.*

Happiness is my family; I don't know how else to say it. Is there a verse reference for that? "He settles the barren women in her home as a happy mother of children" (Ps. 113:9). What greater joy do I have than that? None. There is no greater joy.

I am no perfect mother or wife, but oh, how I love them. And on top of it, to know that my life is being used to shine a light for others. Oh, that's too much! That's boundless joy.

16. Your turn! Use the space below to count your blessings and consider for a moment where true joy comes from:

_____

_____

_____

_____

_____

_____

How might God want you to respond to what he's revealed to you today?

Lesson 20
The Threefold Dream
Part 3: The Plan

Verse of the Day: "You will seek me and find me when you seek me with all your heart." Jeremiah 29:13

The Plan

The third part of God's dream for our lives is that we would find his plan and his purpose for us. For all of us, that is different. Some of us become mothers, instilling hope and a future for the next generation; some never marry, finding their calling as undivided messengers of the gospel or as healers; some minister through work; still others have many irons in the fire, and when put in proper order, they all prosper.

To find his plan and purpose for each of us is not to compare ourselves to the plan and purpose of others. That only trips us up. But to discover our own unique purpose and to actually live it—whether we are facing trial and hardship or enjoying blessing—now that leads to joy.

The Right Companions

We have talked about our True Companion (God) and counterfeit companions. Here we will address right companions.

I am blessed to be married to my best friend. To me, best friends always have your best interest at the center of their hearts. My husband, Shane, has that, and I have that for him. But no relationship is without trial. I am in no position to teach older and wiser women about marriage; rather, it is their position to train me (Titus 2:4). But I do want to share two things that I have learned in the past ten years of being married that do propel me through the good times and bad.

Once when Shane and I were having a particularly frustrating time in our marriage, we went to the bookstore on a date. I wandered over to the Christian section on relationships, picked a random book and opened it; a few sentences seemed to jump off the center of the page—saying essentially that if someone is helping you find God's dreams for your life, then that person is your right companion. At that moment I realized that no matter how difficult things sometimes might be, I was with the person God wanted me to be with. Shane has always supported my dreams and pushed me in the direction of what God dreams for me. From the very first moment he encouraged me to teach a teen Bible study group, to write, to speak, to get rid of my self-centeredness, to be a better mother or better friend—in every way—whether it be hard to hear or not, he has helped me to find God's plan and purpose for my life. And I believe I do the same for him.

1. Think about your closest companion. Are you helping one another find God's dreams for your lives? If so, how? If not, what's preventing you from doing that?

   _____

   _____

   _____

   _____

   _____

Bringing Good and Not Harm

Second, right companions bring good and not harm to one another. When I feel tension at home, I try to ask myself, "Am I bringing good and not harm to my family all the days of my life"? (Prov. 31:12) That verse tells us that every day of our lives we are called to bring good to the ones we love.

Just like unhealthy relationships, healthy relationships are also recognized by their fruit.

Read James 3:13-18.

Here, we see the fruits of an unhealthy relationship again—envy, selfishness, bitterness, and disorder. Ouch! God's plan for us is to get rid of all that! 1 Peter 2:1 says to rid ourselves of "all malice and all deceit, hypocrisy, envy, and slander of every kind."

2. What does James 3:17-18 say are the fruits of a healthy relationship?

_____

_____

_____

3. What do you think God's plan is for your relationships?

_____

_____

_____

4. Are you "bringing good and not harm" to your husband/family/friends? Be honest with yourself here. If the answer is "yes," use the space below to explain how. If the answer is "no," "sometimes," or "maybe," use the space to share how you could change that.

_____

_____

_____

Women who wear crowns of lasting beauty have to live up to them. When I bring harm through my words or actions, I repent in "sackcloth and ashes." My personal experience is that if we treat others with goodness, good will come to us.

God's Part of the Plan and Our Part of the Plan

Read Jeremiah 29:11-14.

Many people know verse 11 by heart but ignore the other part of the verse—our part. I've written it here for your study:

> *"For I know the plans I have for you," declares the Lord, "plans to prosper you and not to harm you, plans to give you hope and a future. Then you will call upon me and come and pray to me, and I will listen to you. You will seek me and find me when you seek me with all your heart. I will be found by you," declares the Lord, "and will bring you back from captivity…and exile."*

5. According to the verse, what is God's part in the plan? Check all that apply:

    ☐ To know the plan
    ☐ To prosper us
    ☐ Not to harm us
    ☐ To listen to us
    ☐ To be found by us
    ☐ To bring us back from captivity
    ☐ To bring us back from exile

6. According to these verses, what is our part in the plan? Check all that apply:

    ☐ To know the plan
    ☐ To seek prosperity
    ☐ To call upon him
    ☐ To come to him
    ☐ To refuse him
    ☐ To pray to him
    ☐ To seek him when times are hard but not seek him when things are going well
    ☐ To seek him with all our hearts

❐ To allow him to release us from captivity and gather us from exile

When I went to Munich, I had a plan to make as much money as possible then travel; but God intercepted that plan with his plan.

7. Have you ever made a plan that you thought would lead to happiness, but it didn't? Explain here:

___

Read Proverbs 16:3, 9.

8. What do these verses say about the best plans for your life?

___

Read Proverbs 19:21.

9. Write Proverbs 19:21 here:

___

10. What do these verses tell you about God's plan for you?

___

His Purpose

When I finally came home after quitting modeling, it was Easter and I was sitting at the long rectangular dinner table with my family in California. My beautiful grandmother, her crown of silver hair resplendent in the candlelight, was on my right. As many—but not all—early twenty-somethings do, I was rambling on with roundabout thinking and confusion about what the plan might be for my life now while family members listened patiently.

Grandma Betty didn't speak up often and never raised her voice unless to squeal with delight that one of her grandchildren had come to visit her. But she kindly interrupted my haphazard musings, and with her Pacific blue eyes dancing with a joy that seemed to never leave her, she said with utter peace, "She will work it out. She will work it out." And that settled the discussion at the table that day.

The truth is God "worked it out" for me. He unveiled his plan for me and continues to unveil it piece-by-piece, step-by-step. So far his dream for me is not about glamour; it's about giving. From the moment my children were born, this dream has involved dying to myself daily to give them all or more of what they need.

The dream has included bringing my husband good and not harm all the days of his life, even when I'm not in the mood! It has meant tireless work for the kingdom, late nights, sacrifice, hard work. But these things give me lasting joy.

> **Highlighted Reading:** "Do you have a perfect dream for your life? It may not be your father's, your mother's, your sister's, or your brother's dream for you. But that's all right…It doesn't matter what other people have dreamt for you. What matters is what God's dreams are for your life. What does he want to 'work out' in you" (p. 130)?

Your Dreams

11. What are some of the dreams you have for your life? Whether we are eighteen or eighty-eight, we all have dreams. What are yours?

12. What do you think are God's dreams for your life?

Your Gifts and Talents

> **Highlighted Reading:** "You can begin discovering God's perfect dream for you by looking at your gifts and talents. What are you good at?…What ignites passion in you? What do you care about? What makes you feel beautiful and worthy, like you are contributing to the earth? It is the answers to these questions that can lead you to the purpose God had for your life when he first formed you" (p. 130).

13. Take the space below to answer the questions in the passage above.

Gifts

Read 1 Corinthians 12:4-11.

14. What do you think your spiritual gifts are? If you are not sure, ask a trusted friend or family member to help you.

Read 1 Corinthians 14:3, 12.

15. What is the purpose of spiritual gifts?

    Check all that apply:
    - ☐ Strengthening
    - ☐ Encouragement
    - ☐ Comfort
    - ☐ Building up the church

Let's not miss that 1 Corinthians 12:7 says that "to each one the manifestation of the Spirit is given for the common good," and all gifts are useless without love (1 Cor. 13:2). Our gifts are gifts that reach beyond ourselves. They are not just for us; they are for the common good and they are intended to strengthen, encourage, comfort, and build up others.

How much do you believe that God gave you specific interests, talents, and gifts because he has a plan to use them to edify (instruct, enlighten, teach, improve) the church through you?

Please make an X on the line below to show how much you believe it:

Believe   Do Not Believe

_____

Talents

Read Matthew 25:14-29.

16. How best do you think you can invest and multiply your talents so that they bless the world around you?

_____

_____

_____

Read 2 Timothy 1:6-7.

17. What are we supposed to "fan into flame"?

    Check one:
    ☐ The number of followers we have on Instagram
    ☐ Our abilities to snap, text, and post faster
    ☐ The gifts God gave us
    ☐ The number of images we see daily
    ☐ The amount of money we have in the bank

18. If the gifts we have are from God, given to us by his Spirit, then what characteristics of that Spirit do we need to draw upon to fan our gifts into flame?

    Check all that apply:
    ☐ Fear that we can't do it
    ☐ Power
    ☐ Love

- ☐ Self-doubt
- ☐ Self-discipline
- ☐ Procrastination and distraction

To be honest, I come to you as someone who lacks self-discipline. I procrastinate; I am so easily distracted that I'll go from one thing to another to another without getting anything done well; I can wallow in self-doubt better than a pig in a pen of warm and muddy poop; I can fan fear into flame until it is a raging fire preventing me from going where God wants me to go. I can do all that and have done it! But all those things quench the full manifestation of the gifts given to me. In 1 Thessalonians 5:19, we are told, "Do not put out the Spirit's fire."

Distraction, procrastination, self-doubt, fear—they all quench the Spirit's fire within us. In order to take part in God's dream for our lives, we have to tap into his power that we can do all things through Christ who strengthens us. We have to channel his spirit of love that drives out fear and delivers us from the bondage of ourselves into the incredible freedom of living out his plan for us.

In this we must learn to imitate our Savior with the self-discipline of dying to ourselves every day.

19. When it comes to your gifts and talents, how would you have to die to yourself daily in order for the full manifestation of the Spirit's power to be fanned into flame in you?

_____

_____

_____

Fanning your gifts into flame is practicing them, honing them, and devoting yourself to their growth—all with the power of the Spirit at work within you. Don't miss that. Fan them, my sweet friend. Fan them!

20. Using the space below, write how you intend to fan your gifts into flame, so that:
    You have invested and multiplied the effect of your talents.
    The church is edified.
    The fire of the Spirit blazes through you.

    _____

    _____

    _____

It is the Lord's purpose that will prevail. His purpose for us is to live out his "Perfect Dream": to know his love and experience the peace and security of walking with him; to allow him to heal our brokenness and bring beauty from the ashes; and to find his plan and purpose for our lives.

This brings us to our sixth truth, which replaces the lie, "If you are successful and rich, you will be happy." This truth comes from the voice of God: "Money and position will never fully satisfy you; you were created for relationship with me, and only discovering my dream for your life will bring you joy."

Truth #6

God says, "Money and position will never fully satisfy you; you were created for relationship with me, and only discovering my dream for your life will bring you joy."

The ultimate joy comes from living out his dream. As you read these last few verses, meditate on the real source of joy.

Joy

Psalm 16:11a: "You have made known to me the path of life; you fill me with joy in your presence."

Luke 2:10b: "I bring you good news of great joy that will be for all the people." [This is the angel of the Lord speaking to the shepherds about the birth of Jesus]

John 16:22: "Now is your time of grief, but I will see you again and you will rejoice, and no one will take away your joy."

Acts 14:17: "Yet he has not left himself without testimony: He has shown kindness by giving you rain from heaven and crops in their seasons; he provides you with plenty of food and fills your hearts with joy."

Acts 13:52: "And the disciples were filled with joy and with the Holy Spirit."

Deuteronomy 16:15b: "For the Lord your God will bless you in all…the work of your hands, and your joy will be complete."

1 Thessalonians 2:19: "For what is our hope, our joy, or the crown in which we will glory in the presence of our Lord Jesus when he comes? Is it not you"?

1 Thessalonians 2:20 (NIV): "Indeed, you are our glory and joy."

As I said in my introduction of *Girl Perfect*, at the very beginning of the journey: My children are the joy. And you, my friend, are my joy and my crown.

> How might God want you to respond to what he's revealed to you today?
>
> _____
>
> _____
>
> _____

Girl Perfect Readings

Chapter 7—The Perfect Escape:
Loneliness, Drugs and Suicide

Chapter 8—The Perfect Path:
The Wide and Narrow Roads

Lessons

21: Captivity and Exile

22: Going Into Hiding: False Methods of Escape

23: The Wide Path or the Narrow?

24: A Little Girl Again

25: The Perfect Path

Lesson 21
Captivity and Exile

Read or reread *Girl Perfect*, Chapter 7, "The Perfect Escape."

Verse of the Day: "Because of the Lord's great love we are not consumed, for his compassions never fail. They are new every morning; great is your faithfulness." Lamentations 3:22-23

I have battled a lot of fear while writing this study, all of which has centered on my own insufficiency. I have been afraid that I am not well-versed enough to know just the right places to lead you in the Word; I have doubted and questioned my own ability; I've thought many times that the real issue is that I'm not as marvelous as other Bible teachers, and who am I to assume I can write a Bible study, anyway?

My feelings of inadequacy have absolutely nothing to do with my calling! None of this has to do with my sufficiency! It has to do with God's. I spend so much time with my face in the Word, my face to the floor, my heart reaching out for the Son of God, that he teaches me a better way—a true way. We have all been called for a time and a purpose of our own. You don't have to—and believe me, don't want to—be me; I don't have to ever hold a candle to any other teacher. The image that God desires to impress upon us is the one we see when we look into his face.

As I've written, I've heard these terrible voices over and over and over again, voices I'm sure you will recognize: "You can't do it! It's not possible. It can't be done. You're not good enough." They remind me of the voices that I heard in those dreams in Munich—accusing voices that said I would never measure up to what the world said I had to be.

As we grow in our faith, we have to learn to recognize voices that lie, and truth must become louder in our ears. "Your love for me is enough, Jen," God has told me. "I will gain the victory. Fight hard; run strong. It is for Olivia, that little girl inside of each of my daughters. Don't give up, and don't give in." The voice of Jesus drowns out the lies of the enemy.

The topics raised in this chapter, and in this entire book for that matter, are far too big for you or me to tackle. It is the working of his mighty strength within that gives me the power to raise and explore the greatest longings of each of our hearts and the false sources we wish would fill them.

Loneliness, depression, self-harm, suicide, drugs—these are issues we press into now. It would be easier not to discuss them. It would be less challenging, as I said at the beginning, just to read the book and walk away—or not even finish, giving up in the middle because it's just too darn hard.

Believe me, here begins the hardest part of the journey. Like the Israelites who had been in captivity for so long, we too have to trust the leadership of God out of confinement and into freedom. I am pressing on and ask you to do the same.

We now delve into the deepest recesses of our hearts—the places where it seems no light can touch. But we are not alone. God goes with us; his Word, our lamp. And he is going to take us out the other side of the canyon. But he doesn't want to take us out the same way we came in. We entered one way; he desires we leave another.

Lie #7
If you are in pain, the things
of the world will bring you peace.

The Longing:
Peace

Peace

The lie which says, "If you are in pain, the things of the world will bring you peace," tells us that a host of things will make us feel better when we are alone, afraid, confused, lost, and longing. Certainly this was the lie I believed when I lived in Munich.

> **Highlighted Reading:** "Mom, this is not my home," I tried to explain to her on the phone the next day. "It's like I'm a visitor here; nothing is mine" (p. 143).

The longing for peace is a longing to "go home." The backyard of my youth was my Canaan, my land of plenty and promise. Each one of us has a Canaan in our hearts; a home where we know we will be at peace if we could just return there.

In my case, I chose to leave that place of peace and travel far and wide in search of what would fill me; now, I longed to return. I longed for freedom from the chains that weighed me down and threatened to bury me in those deep waters.

As we read in the Book of Genesis, God's people enjoyed his favor in the land of Canaan, the profuse bounty of a land flowing with milk and honey. But division in Joseph's family drove Joseph out of that place, and he landed in Egypt. There, due to centuries of rule under those who did not honor God, slavery came to God's people. For four hundred years, they remained in captivity.

Let's review the definition of *captivity:* "taken and held as if a prisoner; held under control of another but having the appearance of independence."

Held Under the Control of Another

Read John 8:34.

1. Write it here:

   _____

   _____

Read Romans 6:16.

2. According to these verses, how can we become slaves?

   _____

   _____

   _____

3. Whose control do you think we are under when sin is our master?

   _____

   _____

Read Romans 7:5.

4. What is the fruit of sin?

   _____

From the time I left my personal Canaan, I was a slave to sin, under the control of it; it was my master, and I bore fruit for "death."

Read Jeremiah 8:5.

This is God's cry to his people, saying to Jerusalem, "You know me; yet turn away from me, why"?

5. What does it say here they cling to?

   _____

When both Shane and I believed the lie that drugs and alcohol would bring us peace, we were clinging to deceit, and that bore fruit for death. That separation from God made us both, in our very separate worlds, long to return to home, the land of peace, hope, and a future.

6. Have you ever "clung to deceit," believing that something would bring you peace and finding out that it only brought a slow death to your soul? Using the space below for private reflection, write about it:

_____
_____
_____
_____
_____
_____
_____

Read Isaiah 30:12-13.

7. Is there something you are enslaved to, that you know deep down is becoming like a "high, cracked wall" between you and your land of Canaan, the abundant life that God wants for you? Use the space below to name it before him:

_____
_____
_____
_____
_____

Exile

Read Jeremiah 29:11-14 again, giving special attention to verse 14.

8. What does God want to bring his people back from? Circle all that apply:

    Captivity   Exile   Banishment

This verse has a very literal interpretation. Jeremiah had been warning God's people of a coming judgment, which would involve the destruction of Jerusalem and their exile as a result of their idolatry and disobedience. The promise in these verses reveals that God's heart was to redeem and restore them.

So this is a literal prophecy that we often use for a figurative application. If we are going to think of these verses in a figurative sense, then what do the captivity, banishment, and exile represent? As one who feels in her heart that she was released from "captivity," "gathered from the nations," and brought back from a place of "exile," my question then is, what exiles us into places of loneliness? The answer is obvious, though hard to hear: our sin becomes like a wall, high and cracked, that makes us feel separated from him, far from home. In essence, we banish ourselves. We pursue our own course, a counterfeit peace (Jer. 8:6).

Let's read the definitions of exile and banishment: *exile:* a state of absence from one's country or home. *banishment:* to remove from a home or place of usual resort.

Most people focus on the positive part of Jeremiah 29:11-14, but few bring up the captivity and exile. It sounds better just to say he's got great plans for us, doesn't it? But let's be careful to apply all of the literal meaning to all of the figurative meaning; to remember that idolatry and disobedience were the reason why the people of Jerusalem were in exile, and to remember that not only does God have great plans for you, but part of that plan is to deliver you from your slavery, your "captivity." But like the believers in John 8:33, who refused to see themselves as slaves, we too must admit that we have been slaves first so we can be set free.

Idolatry

Read Romans 1:25.

9. Idolatry is worshipping and serving "created things rather than the Creator." It is expecting the things of the world to bring us the peace we long for. When we do this, for what do we exchange the truth of God?

_____

Read Isaiah 44:6-45:8.

10. In these verses, God draws a sharp contrast between himself, the "Creator," and idols, "created things." Drawing upon Isaiah 44 and 45, use the space below to list the distinct characteristics that differentiate God and idols.

God   Idols

_____
_____
_____
_____
_____

Taking a look at your list, answer this question: Can the things of this world bring you peace? My friend, in your heart you know the answer. It wasn't until I admitted to myself: "I am feeding on ashes; a deluded heart misleads me; this thing in my right hand is a lie;" and threw away my idols that I experienced the great return home to my Creator (Isa. 44:20). And he said to me, "I have swept away your offenses like a cloud, your sins like the morning mist. Return to me, for I have redeemed you" (44:22).

Some real life examples of idolatry—the bowing down to created things rather than the Creator – are: the use of sorcery, tarot cards, palm readers, and the like; the worship of man; the worship of yourself, including self-gratification being more important than gratifying the will of God; the use of drugs or alcohol; sexual sin; dependence on food, money, shopping, or possessions to bring you peace; and finding escape in what we know in our hearts is evil and wrong. There are so many ways that we can choose counterfeit gods.

11. What counterfeit gods do you need to throw out? In what ways are you feeding on ashes and your deluded heart is misleading you? Use the space below to lay your idols at his feet and to say, "These things cannot save me! I admit that I am a slave to them."

_____

_____

_____

_____

_____

Read Isaiah 30:19-22.

12. When you cry for help, what does God say he will do? (v. 19)

_____

_____

My friend, when we throw out our idols like a menstrual cloth and say, "Away with you!" he sweeps away our offenses like the morning mist. He is the Lord, and there is no other; he answers our every cry. He receives you with compassion, mercy, and abounding love.

Finally, read Lamentations 3:17-26.

"Because of the Lord's great love we are not consumed, for his compassions never fail. They are new every morning…It is good to wait quietly for the salvation of the Lord." (Lam. 3:22-23, 26)

How might God want you to respond to what he's revealed to you today?

_____

_____

_____

Close your time today in prayer.

Lesson 22
Going Into Hiding:
False Methods of Escape

Verse of the Day: "My peace I give you. I do not give to you as the world gives. Do not let your hearts be troubled and do not be afraid." John 14:27

> **Highlighted Reading:** "I...took a few drags off a leftover joint, and crawled into bed. Even though it was still daylight, I pulled the covers over my head...I nestled even further under the covers, read a few pages of my vampire novel, and drifted off to sleep" (p. 140).

1. Believing the lie that the things of this world will bring us peace, we become enslaved to them. In the last lesson I asked you to list the differences between God and idols, and to name your own idols. When you trust idols to bring you peace, what happens?

   _____

   _____

   _____

> **Highlighted Reading:** "'I don't want to live my life like this,' I cried, my eyes filling with tears. I slid to the ground, curling into a ball, sobbing. It was as if someone had taken my heart and wrung it out like a rag...My head hurt. My mouth and eyes hurt. My heart hurt" (pp. 141, 144).

We are longing for peace, but when we run to things to fill the longing—whether it's food or drugs or sleep or men—they may numb the pain for a moment, but ultimately we are "feeding on ashes," and they squeeze the life out of our little-girl hearts. As I say in the book, "It's not where you are; it's *whom* you run *to* that counts" (p. 150).

2. To what or to whom do you run when you are in pain?

3. Is this method of escape healthy or unhealthy for you? Why?

As Job 13:4 says, lies are worthless physicians. So why do so many of us look to everything but God to be the anesthesia? Why do we inject false painkillers into the greatest wounds of our little-girl hearts? Because the world tells us to; it promises it can ease the pain. But the world lies.

Only truth can set us free.

Depression

When I was in Munich, I believe I was suffering from what the clinical world calls *short-term depression*. Short-term depression can be caused by personal loss or trauma. Chronic, or long-term depression, is often caused by trauma in childhood, which can include emotional, physical, or sexual abuse; yelling or threats of abuse; neglect; criticism; inappropriate or unclear expectations; maternal separation; familial conflict or addiction; violence in the family, neighborhood, or TV; racism and poverty. There actually may be a genetic basis to some depression as well, but even if there is that genetic propensity, it is usually triggered by some traumatic or stressful event.[1]

Women are twice as likely to become depressed as men. I am no doctor, but I wonder if the reason for this is that women hear twice the lies about themselves and are twice as likely to believe them. The travesty is that nearly two-thirds of the women suffering from depression do not get the help they need.[2] I believe this is the case because women are taught to wear masks. It's not acceptable for us to walk into church, school, or work, and say, "Help!"

But here we are taking off the masks. Symptoms of depression include feeling persistently sad; losing interest in your life; excessive crying; feelings of worthlessness; sleeping too much or too little; appetite loss; decreased energy; thoughts of death or suicide; and difficulty making decisions or concentrating.[3] In essence, depression is a negative view of our world, ourselves, and our future.[4]

The Avalanche

> **Highlighted Reading:** "It seems to happen all at once, like a landslide...I am falling, and the rocks and boulders start rushing so fast they carry me away in their current... When I land at the bottom...I am battered and beaten. I feel broken all over" (pp. 135-136).

4. Have you ever had an avalanche in your life or seen someone you love in an avalanche like this that leaves you or them feeling broken all over? Please describe it. You always have the option of keeping what you write here private. But remember, the more we open up and share our experiences, the more the women and girls around us will feel that they are not alone in theirs.

The primary ingredient in effective depression recovery is the establishment of good relationships. Studies show that relationships with partners, teachers, co-workers, and a supportive social network result in physical and emotional healing, happiness, and life satisfaction, and prevent isolation and loneliness, which are major factors in depression.[5] We are not meant to be alone, isolated, and in "exile." We are meant to be in community and in communion with our Creator and his people.

The best medicine for depression is a good therapist or physician, and a good community. I believe this community must be a spiritual one in which we are taught to fill the hole in our hearts with our hearts' Creator. But this begins with "crying out in the crowd," pushing in for the Healer, taking off the masks and saying, "I know you'll heal me." It begins with getting real and getting help. If you struggle with feelings of depression like the ones I listed earlier, I encourage you to get the help you need. Speak up and speak out.

Church, let's open up our arms and our hearts to the hurting. And let's not forget: look people directly in the eyes, the windows of the soul. Maybe there you will see their soul hunger.

Self-Harm

Self-harm is one of the most upsetting trends among young people. It's not something fun to talk about, but we must talk about it because the issue is rearing its ugly head in this generation, and we are called to bring truth and hope to this generation.

STUDY GUIDE

Read Psalm 78:1-8.

5. What is our responsibility to the next generation?

6. Why are we supposed to teach the younger generation the wonders of God?

Read Deuteronomy 4:9 and 39-40.

These are the words God said to his people before they crossed the Jordan to take possession of Canaan, the promised land.

7. What result will teaching God's commands to our children produce? (4:40)

We are commanded to declare God's wonderful works, passing them down through the generations, so that life will go well for us and for them. So if something is damaging our children or our children's children, we had better be addressing it and speaking truth to it.

Self-harm is very confusing to the older generation, yet it is becoming commonplace among the younger. Self-harm includes any behavior intended to provide relief from emotional pain or emotional numbness through self-inflicted physical trauma. The most common form of self-harm is skin cutting. Another prevalent form is burning or branding; others are scratching, rubbing, pulling one's hair out, and banging one's head.

Young women are the most common self-injurers. Risk factors to self-injury are environmental (including growing up in an invalidating environment which may or may not include abuse), biological (having a predisposition to emotional dysfunction), and behavioral (substance abuse, being involved in unhealthy relationships, etc.).[6] Self-injurers often suffer from negative self-esteem, hypersensitivity to rejection, and suppressed anger. Most people who self-injure tend to be perfectionists who haven't learned how to handle intense feelings and haven't learned to express their feelings verbally. That pretty much describes the issues of the generation, doesn't it?

Many, though not all, teens and young adults with self-harm issues have experienced some form of past trauma resulting in ongoing emotional distress. Instead of expressing this pain in productive ways—for instance, talking about it—many of these young people repress it. Many young people who have coped by repressing their feelings eventually have difficulty feeling anything. Therefore, to feel, they cut.

One reason that teens may turn to physical pain as a coping strategy is that they are terrified of emotional pain and are afraid that it might overwhelm them. Others use cutting to redirect their attention from overwhelming emotions because it seems like a way to control their pain. Cutting is addictive because, like any drug, the brain's chemical reactions to cutting wear off and the cutter must do it again and again to feel relief.[7]

It is an evil escape tactic when we turn on ourselves. Drug abuse; alcoholism; bingeing and purging; anorexia; self-inflicted obesity; allowing ourselves to abused; rejecting our gender; cutting and any self-harm—it is all turning on ourselves. And when we turn against our very selves, body and soul, we are not turning to the One who made us, loves us, and can truly help us.

STUDY GUIDE

Jesus Heals a Cutter

Read Mark 5:1-15.

8. Note that the evil spirit within the man called himself "Legion," which was the largest unit of the Roman army, consisting of three thousand to six thousand soldiers. Clearly this man was possessed by many, many demons. Use the space below to respond to what you've read through writing down a prayer.

_____

_____

_____

_____

It is very telling that this generation is using cutting as an escape mechanism from emotional pain. Cutting oneself is demonic. It is taking the wounds, the stripes, the beating Christ took for us, and imposing it upon ourselves.

Read Isaiah 53:5.

9. What does this say to the cutter?

_____

_____

_____

As 1 Peter 2:24 says, "He himself bore our sins on his body on the tree." There is no need for us to bear them. Yes, "the punishment that brought us peace was upon him" and "by his wounds we are healed" (Isa. 53:5). If self-harm is a way to deal with repressed emotional pain, my question is: Why doesn't this generation feel that they can speak about their pain?

A careful reading of my book will show that during my time of exile and captivity to sin, I also felt unheard by my family. It was then that I "allowed my fingernails to catch fire," desired to burn myself in the bathtub, and ultimately considered suicide.

When we, as children, feel as if we need to project the perfect image for our families, we crumble beneath the masks. We want to be truthful, but we can't. We want to be real, but the older generation isn't. We want to say what hurts and be met without judgment. We want to be received and don't want to be rejected, so instead of speaking up and risking judgment, we stuff down our feelings; we remain silent, burying our sadness and pain.

Because there are higher incidences of eating disorders, gender-dysphoria, self-harm, depression, suicide, and drug abuse among the children of this generation, the people of God had better wake up and make themselves more accessible. We had better stop acting so shocked when a young person gets real. We had better encourage realness, talk about the tough stuff in church and at home, and give our young people avenues for healthy ways to express their emotional pain. If they feel that they can't speak of their pain, it will get locked up inside and they are apt to turn on themselves.

Anything that violates the precious, hand-knit creations of God is evil. How it must grieve our Father so, especially because he sent his Son to take all the injury on his body for us to save us from punishing ourselves.

Suicide

We are going to instill truth into the topic of suicide. We all know the numbers are on the rise; that depression can lead to it; that self-harm can be, but is not always, linked to it; and that unchecked mental illness can definitely contribute to it. Because a dear one I knew did this, I also want to add a word of extreme caution that a person should never abruptly stop taking his or her anti-depression or bi-polar medication, as that too can lead to psychosis and ultimately taking one's precious life.

As I am writing this, I just learned that a 24-year-old girl closely linked to our family killed herself. If you or anyone you know is having suicidal thoughts, you need to call your local crisis center open 24/7 if you become overwhelmed and if it is NOT an emergency. Call 911 if it is. You can also make an action plan with numbers you can call should you feel overwhelmed and carry them with you. There are wonderful free referral services that are readily available. Please refer to www.girlperfectbook.com for a list of free counseling referral services. Call out and get help, because tomorrow, the sun will come up and there is a new day of hope.

Regarding my own experience with suicidal thoughts, I want to make it clear that I have never been clinically depressed. Growing up, I always placed great value on my life; I had love around me as a child and would have never dreamt that life would get so overwhelming that suicide would cross my mind.

I remember very well what happened when I was in the bathtub in Munich and how my life and mind were haunted by evil spirits. Not only did I paint a hell-like scene on a canvas in that apartment and began reading vampire novels, but I can also still see in my mind's eye the "shadowy spirits that danced on the tiles," shooting out of the red water bottle I had painted. Evil spirits were present in that bathroom; I know it.

I say this to point out that suicide is evil, of the devil, and not anywhere close to the goodness of our loving, mighty Savior of a God. The good news is that I chose love. I chose life. I chose to hope in something I couldn't see—that things would turn around and that life would be worth living.

Jesus came so that we might have life, and life to the full (John 10:10). My friend, after all this darkness, I have life to the full. He raised me from those waters in new life, and he can do that for you, your daughter, and your granddaughter. That's the truth. Pass it on.

Hope for the Hurting

We are going to close this challenging day of study with some hope for the hurting and with truth to set us free!

Read these verses and let them sink into your soul:

Amos 5:6 (NLT): "Come back to me and live!"

Joel 2:12-14 (NLT): "Turn to me now while there is time! Give me your hearts. Come with fasting, weeping, and mourning. Don't tear your clothing in your grief; instead, tear your hearts. Return to the Lord your God for he is merciful and compassionate, slow to get angry and filled with unfailing love. He is eager to relent and not punish. Who knows? Perhaps he will give you a reprieve, sending you a blessing. "

Romans 12:21 (NLT): "Don't let evil conquer you, but conquer evil by doing good."

Read Psalm 30.

10. Use the space below to answer the psalmist's question, what gain is there in our destruction, in our going down into the pit? Why is it God's will for us to live?

___

___

___

11. When he removes our sackcloth, our garments of despair, what does he clothe us with? (v. 11)

___

The Longing for Peace

Read John 14:27 and 16:33.

12. What do these verses say to you about the source of our peace?

_____

_____

_____

_____

To the sinful woman of Luke 7, Jesus said, "Your sins are forgiven…Your faith has saved you; go in peace" (7:48-50). To the bleeding woman of Mark 5, he said, "Daughter, your faith has healed you. Go in peace and be freed from your suffering" (5:34). To you, he says, "My peace I give to you; my peace I leave with you."

13. Who is he who grants peace and freedom from suffering? Who is he who grants salvation and forgiveness of sin? Who is he? Write his name here:

_____

Our seventh truth, which replaces the lie, "The things of the world will bring you peace," is simple: "Only Jesus brings peace."

Truth #7
Only Jesus brings peace.

How might God want you to respond to what he's revealed to you today?

_____

_____

_____

Lesson 23
The Wide Path or The Narrow?

Read or reread *Girl Perfect*, Chapter 8, "The Perfect Path."

Verse of the Day: "Since the first day that you set your mind to gain understanding and to humble yourself before your God, your words were heard, and I have come in response to them." Daniel 10:12

Lie #8
The wide road has much more to
offer and leads to satisfaction.

The Longing:
Direction

The wide road can look so attractive. The people on the wide road can look so attractive! But we know from the garden that just because something looks good doesn't mean it is good. We must believe God's Word. His Word is truth (John 17:17). He does not lie (Num. 23:19). So anything that directly contradicts God's truth is a lie. Therefore, "the wide road has much more to offer and leads to satisfaction" is a lie. But the problem is this lie is so accepted by the world that it is even hard for Christians to fully resist it.

Because lies lead us into captivity, preventing us from experiencing the abundant life, it is essential for us to learn to recognize a lie and replace it with truth. Why? Because truth sets us free, and that's what we are really after when we are calling out for direction—freedom.

With each lie comes a longing, and in the case of the wide and narrow roads, the longing is for direction. There are so many different avenues we can go down in the world; which one do we take? Naturally, the world's avenue to satisfaction turns out to be not as satisfying as it promises. God's avenue to satisfaction is far different but faithfully leads us where our hearts long to go.

The Choice

Read Matthew 7:13-14.

1. Write Matthew 7:13-14 here:

> **Highlighted Reading:** "I've dressed and chosen to go for a walk in the park, kind of the way one chooses life over death" (p. 155).

Just as choosing not to do drugs and alcohol is up to us, just as choosing healthy methods of escape— like taking a walk in the park—is up to us, so the choice is ours whether we take the wide road or the narrow. The lie that says the wide road has more to offer is very deceptive because it makes it sound as if rejecting Christ is a viable option for us.

I know the wide road really well because I spent many years on it. I know what it looks like, smells like, feels like, tastes like. What the average person doesn't realize is that they are literally choosing death when they choose the wide road. Why would anyone choose death?

Read 2 Corinthians 4:1-4.

2. Who is the "god of this age"?

   _____

3. What does this verse say he has done to the minds of unbelievers?

   _____

   _____

4. What are unbelievers unable to see?

   _____

   _____

Because the minds of unbelievers have been blinded by the "the god of this age," that nasty and pathetic serpent, they can't see clearly. Specifically, they cannot see the "light of the gospel of the glory of Christ, who is the image of God." They might believe in a god, or they might believe that "Jesus was a prophet, among many good prophets," but not that he was the living representation of God and that faith in his name brings forgiveness of sin.

To some, statements like "all roads lead to God" sound like very reasonable ideas, especially considering the wide variety of world religions. But if the Word is truth, the real issue—no matter how wonderful those people are—is they can't see the light of the gospel. They have been blinded; their vision is veiled; and the only one who can remove the veil is Christ himself.

Read 1 John 5:1-12.

5. Who has overcome the world?

   _____

6. What does this say we call God if we do not believe his testimony about his Son? (v. 10)

7. What does this say is the difference between he who has the Son and he who does not have the Son? (v. 12)

_____

_____

_____

The lie is so loud that it muffles the truth that we are talking about a life or death decision here. Choosing the wide road or the narrow is about accepting or rejecting an invitation to eternity with God. Who in their right mind would reject eternity with God? No one—that's the problem. They are not in their "right minds"; their minds have been blinded by the lord of the air, the prince of the earth, the god of the age.

8. How do Jesus's words about the wide and narrow roads directly contradict the statement that "all roads lead to God"?

_____

_____

_____

The Wide Road

> **Highlighted Reading:** "I looked around at the table scattered with a lighter, a mess of tobacco leaves, and rolling papers, and at the dark night out the window...*The wide road*, I realized. *This is the wide road*" (p. 158).

9. Do you truly believe that choosing the wide road—a way of life in rebellion and disobedience to God's Word—leads to destruction? Put an X on the line below to represent how

much you believe it. Tell the truth. (That's what we do here.)

Do Not Believe   Believe Fully

_____

From Genesis to Malachi, the recurring theme of God's people in the Old Testament is this: they enjoy his favor and blessing; then they forget they need him, become rebellious, and their sin leads them into captivity. Desperate for his favor again, they cry out to him. Faithful to his promises, God delivers them. Obedient to him again, they enjoy once again a time of blessing... Then they forget about him and the whole cycle repeats itself. It's pretty ridiculous.

In the time of Jeremiah, the people had once again rejected God and were in captivity. Jeremiah prophesied that God would not allow the captives to return to their homeland of Jerusalem for seventy years. Knowing this time period was about to end, the prophet Daniel pled with God in prayer, petition, and fasting to take his people back. As you read the following passage, look for words that signify what resulted from the people "going their own way."

Read Daniel 9:1-13.

10. Where did their rebellion lead them?

_____

_____

11. What was the result of "transgressing [God's] law and turning away, refusing to obey him"? (vv. 11-14)

    Circle all that apply:
    A. They had a lot of fun!
    B. They had a wide range of experiences.
    C. They encountered great disaster.
    D. They experienced shame and desolation.

Daniel admitted, "We have not sought the favor of the LORD our God by turning from our sins and giving attention to your truth" (v. 13). With great humility and ownership of sin, he fully admitted that disaster and desolation was the result.

> **Highlighted Reading:** "The choices we make, the routes we take, lead to destinations that can often not be reversed. We *cannot* go back" (p. 157).

12. Using the space below, list some good choices you have made and list some bad choices that you have made. Then list the consequences of those choices.

    Good Choices   Bad Choices

    _____   _____
    _____   _____
    _____   _____

    Consequences   Consequences

    _____   _____
    _____   _____
    _____   _____

After Daniel's repentant prayer, God responded by giving Daniel a revelation in the form of an amazing vision which foretold the Anointed One, Jesus, the gate that leads to the narrow road (Dan. 9:20-27). Daniel knew his people were on the wide road and that it led to destruction, and he asked for the path that would lead them to the light. God swiftly answered.

STUDY GUIDE

Read Daniel 10:1-19, Daniel's vision of Jesus.

13. When Daniel cried out to God, in essence saying, "Going our way has led to destruction," God answered him with a picture of Christ. Why do you think God did that?

_____

_____

_____

> **Highlighted Reading:** "But what we can do is jump over to a better path. Turning from darkness to light *is* possible...It begins with the courage to say, 'This path has led me to a dark place, and I want to walk in the light. *Take me to the light, God*'" (p. 157).

Oh, how vast is the difference between the wide and narrow roads!

14. What road are you on? If your answer is the narrow one, have you always walked the narrow road? Or have you at one time walked the wide road and "jumped over to a better path"? If your answer is the wide road, you will receive no judgment from me; I was there. Whatever path you are on, use the space below to tell where you think it is leading.

_____

_____

_____

_____

In Daniel 10:12, God's messengers told Daniel, "Since the first day that you set your mind to gain understanding and to humble yourself before your God, your words were heard." This is the same message we read in Isaiah 30:19, "As soon as he hears, he will answer you." It's the same for us: no matter what we have done, what terrible choices we have made, or how we have rejected God's ways, *from the first moment we set our minds to gain understanding and humble ourselves before him, our words are heard.* Coming from one who did just that, I think that is the most wonderful discovery— that God hears our cries from our first breath of humility. It is his delight to save us, no matter what miserable wretches we have been!

God responded to Daniel by sending him an angel to tell him about the "Book of Truth" (10:21). Angels are "ministering spirits sent to serve those who will inherit salvation" (Heb. 1:14).

Many people who have heard my testimony have told me that the girl I met in Siena, the man I met on the street in Munich, and the man who gave me the Bible in the park were angels. I believe this is quite possible because I remember the clear, unadulterated kindness in their eyes. Even their names suggest it could be so; the people I met in the park were named Michael, Miriam, and Stephen. The girl who gave me the Bible at the little brick church was named Naomi. And I can hardly wait for you to meet Josef in the next chapter!

Regardless of what form the voice of the Shepherd comes in, however, we are to follow his voice when he calls.

Read Daniel 12:1-3.

The angel explained that at the very end of days, there would be a great spiritual battle and that in the end, "Everyone whose name is found written in the book will be delivered. Multitudes who sleep in the dust of the earth will awake; some to everlasting life, others to shame and everlasting contempt." No matter what our beliefs or experiences are, when it's all said and done, there will be Jesus, the Anointed One. Those who reject him will go one way—to destruction—and those with the wisdom to accept him will go the other—to everlasting life. Eternal darkness or eternal light: that's the choice.

Picture It!

15. Using the space below, make a list of adjectives that you think describe everlasting darkness and everlasting light:

    Everlasting Light   Everlasting Darkness

    _____

    _____

    _____

    _____

    _____

    _____

So here it is: we enter the narrow road through a narrow gate, Jesus. We enter the wide road the easy way, our way, But over time the wide road narrows and narrows, becoming more and more obscure and increasingly confining along the way, until the shadows lead us to the edge of darkness and finally into the depths of gloom, the blackest black imaginable, the deepest and most wicked suffering, and we burn there forever.

The narrow road, on the other hand, is not as easy at first; we stumble and fall along the way, but there is always One who picks us up, brushes us off, and carries us through trials; over time, the path widens and widens, becoming richer and more bountiful all the time, until our earthly bodies become spiritual ones and the passageway before us launches into a great expanse of light—true riches, eternal joy, angels singing, heaven, perfection—becoming so brilliant, luminous, and endlessly vast that it is God Almighty in all his glory, forever and ever.

16. Using the space below, draw a picture of the wide and narrow roads, including their entryways and destinations:

The people who shared Christ with me had a conviction about the destinations of the wide and narrow roads. Because they believed that Jesus was the "way, the truth, and the life," that "no one comes to the Father except through him" (John 14:6), they saved my earthly life from being dead and fruitless and they saved my spiritual life for eternity.

As we close this day of study, I give you two choices:

Choice 1: If you know deep down that you are living the life of the wide road, I present to you a choice today to choose the narrow one. Maybe you have already "accepted Jesus"; maybe you haven't. But deep down you know you are walking the wide road. Today I ask you to admit that it leads to destruction and that choosing your own way—in whatever your circumstance—is not going to lead you to the life you really want.

Pray this prayer with me today: Dear God, I have gone the wrong way. I want to jump over to your path, and I want you to lead the way for me. I can't do it without you. Take me to the narrow road, the road that leads to life. I put my faith in you Jesus, for you to lead me where my heart truly wants to go. Don't let me go my own way anymore; it leads to desolation. I want your way, your life, your path, your plan. In Jesus's name, amen.

Choice 2: I want you to bring before the throne someone you love who is on the wide road.

> How might God want you to respond to what he's revealed to you today?
>
> _____
>
> _____
>
> _____

Lesson 24
A Little Girl Again

Verse of the Day: "The old has gone; the new has come!" 2 Corinthians 5:17b

Coming back to Christ is coming back to our little-girl hearts. That's been the purpose of the journey all along. We have swum through torrid and sometimes overwhelming waters. But now is the time to come up for air!

A New Creation

> **Highlighted Reading:** "A breeze stirred, touching my forehead. 'Come in,' I whispered. 'Come in, Jesus.' It was as if that little girl inside me tiptoed through the house of my heart and quietly opened the door to him. As she opened it, the first gray cloud exited, the wind carried it away, and light streamed in. I inhaled a long, fresh, clean breath" (p. 166).

When we open the door to the invitation of Christ, he fills our souls with his breath. Through the Holy Spirit, he fills us with new life. We become "born again," brand new. But we have to be careful that this term "born again" doesn't become commonplace for us, hence losing its true meaning.

Read John 3:1-8.

1. What can we see once we are born again? (v. 3)

   _____

2. What do you think it means to be "born of the Spirit"? (vv. 5-8)

Read 2 Corinthians 5:17.

3. What do you think it means to be "a new creation"?

4. What does "the old has gone, the new has come" mean?

Coming to Him Like a Child

Read Luke 8:40-42 and 49-55.

5. What returned to the little girl when Jesus said, "My child, get up"?

Read Luke 18:16-17

6. Write Luke 18:17 here:

To be born again is to be dead and buried to the old life and to be raised as a little child again, with the Spirit of Christ hoisting you from death to life. To be born again is to become a child again.

> **Highlighted Reading:** "I began wedging my arms in and out, in and out, making angels in the snow just as I used to do in the sand as a girl. I would comb the white crystals with my hands while I listened to the deafening roar of the waves pounding the shore. Wearing my blue and white polka-dot bathing suit, I would play on the beach for hours...[I would] chase the waves, laugh, let them catch me on their way back, and squeal from the cold water washing over my feet..." (pp. 166-167).

At this point of the study, if you say you are a Christian, this should mean that you've actually been "born again." You should have died to your old self and been raised in the new life of the Spirit. For some of us, there is an exact moment, like mine on the German mountain Zugspitze—and even this was only my first "rebirth." For others, there is a time span in which you let go of your former life and turned to God. At that time, "the veil" was removed. There was a transfiguration in you as he revealed himself to you; and during that time, he inwardly passed your soul from death to life anew.

To come to him as a little child again is so very important. We must return to that state of innocence and purity, the backyards of our youth again; to our own lands of Canaan. And we must die to the chains that weighed us down in the world and leave them in the grave.

Dead to the Old

Read Romans 6:1-4.

7. Describe here the old life you died to or are dying to now.

What does God want you to leave in the grave?

The Waters of Baptism

Read Luke 3:21-22.

8. What descended upon Jesus in his baptism?

As we pass from death to life, we too are baptized with the Spirit of God. He is the water that we pass through, the water that cleanses and washes away our sin. That is why water baptism is so important: it symbolizes the passing of our souls from death to life, from dying with Christ to being raised with Christ. We are first baptized "in the water and the Spirit" at the moment we come to him as little children, and we are born again at the moment he fills us with his Spirit through faith in his name. Then we obey him by being water baptized to publicly proclaim that we have passed from death to life.

Jesus is the water that we pass through that *makes us all new.*

9. Now is the time to come back to that little girl inside of you. Using the space below, describe her again—that one made new, the born again you. Get in touch with her innocence again. Get in touch with who she is, who you would be if every single sin were washed away from your soul. What would the little girl do? Would she run? Would she play? Describe her here, giving as much detail as possible:

STUDY GUIDE

The Crossing of the Red Sea

Read Exodus 14:21-31.

This is the first crossing of water the Israelites experienced on their journey out of slavery into Egypt. As the Israelites crossed the Red Sea on dry land, their slave masters pursued them with a vengeance.

10. Who dies in this scene?

11. Who is delivered into a new life of freedom from slavery?

As Nehemiah 9:11 says, "You divided the sea before them, so that they passed through it on dry ground, but you hurled their pursuers into the depths, like a stone into mighty waters."

Leave your bookmark in Exodus and turn to Ezekiel.

Read Ezekiel 28:6-8, the punishment God declared upon the King of Tyre.

12. Write verse 8 here:

_____

_____

_____

Now I must tell you my original title for *Girl Perfect*: *In Mezzo Al Mare*. It means "in the middle of the sea." This title came from the transition I experienced from death to life when I became born again on Mt. Zugspitze. I was later water baptized in the sea of my youth, the Pacific, about a year after I came home from Europe. At the time, I had no idea that our slave masters are drowned in the heart of the seas; all I knew was that I was raised in new life. Now I know that In Mezzo Al Mare is the victory of Jesus for all of us: that through the miracle of Christ on the cross, our slave masters have been hurled into the heart of the sea, never to come up for air.

Read Exodus 15:1-21, the song of Moses and Miriam.

13. What did Miriam do to celebrate? (v. 20)

_____

_____

_____

So get out your tambourine, girlfriend! If you received Christ, your slave masters have been hurled into the depths! Die to that old life of slavery and be raised as a free woman!

Our transition from death to life begins with faith like little children, who believe the simple truth that by receiving Christ we will see the kingdom of God. Over time, he teaches us that he will destroy the enemy in our wake; he makes a way for us to pass

STUDY GUIDE

from the old ways of captivity to a new life, a life where we no longer feed on lies but instead feed on truth—truth that sets us free to be the girls God made us to be.

> How might God want you to respond to what he's revealed to you today?

Lesson 25
The Perfect Path

Verse of the Day: "Ask for the ancient paths, ask where the good way is, and walk in it, and you will find rest for your souls." Jeremiah 6:16

Coming to Christ is to be born again, but that certainly doesn't mean the little girl inside of us has it all figured out as soon as she passes through the gate of the narrow road. Personally, I knew nothing about the ways of God when I came to Christ, except that he could save me. At the point of salvation, all we've done is pass through the gate! Hallelujah for that!

1. Be like Miriam and praise God for your salvation! Praise him here:

> **Highlighted Reading:** "So I prayed that whatever path God wanted me to take would be obvious...I trusted the route would be laid out for me. I did not worry anymore about which road to take" (pp. 163-164).

---

2. How does following the narrow road fill our longing for direction in life?

Read Isaiah 51:10 and 15-16.

3. As we walk the narrow road, what does God cover us with?

Read Isaiah 52:12.

4. As we walk the narrow road, where is the Lord?

Read Psalm 119:105.

5. As we walk the narrow road, what lights the way?

6. Draw a picture of where he is in relation to you:

The Path of His Presence

Following the narrow road is realizing we are on the "Path of His Presence." We are not alone. He covers us with the shadow of his hand; he goes before us and behind us; and his Word lights the way. What path could be better than that? None.

Read Exodus 13:21-22.

7. When God was leading the Israelites out of slavery and into the Red Sea, how did he show them he was with them?

   _____

   _____

When the Egyptians, their former masters, pursued them, the Israelites became seized with fear.

Read Exodus 14:19-20.

8. What did God's presence do then?

   _____

   _____

   _____

The Lord literally comes between his people and the enemy. As he reconciles us to himself, he literally separates us from our past.

Read Romans 8:35-39.

9. The enemy looks at us like sheep to be slaughtered, but nothing can separate us from the love of God that is ours in Christ Jesus our Lord. How does this make you feel?

   _____

_____

_____

As we walk the narrow road, we walk the path of his Presence. He goes before us and behind us; he separates us from the enemy while uniting us with his love; and he guides us as a gentle shepherd.

The Path of the Shepherd

We have so much to learn after that initial "passing through the sea." Many of us, myself included, learn the hard way. Some of us bring the slavery of our pasts along with us, which frustrates, confuses, and slows our march to freedom. Others are just pig-headed sheep and won't listen to the Shepherd. I've done both. I know from personal experience that these strongholds—idolatry and disobedience—strongly hold us back from entering the fullness of what God has for us, what I like to think of as the promised land.

> **Highlighted Reading:** "The book was small and could fit in the palm of my hand; its pages were thin and browned with age. Someone had taken care to reinforce the cover by gluing a photograph of a pasture to the front and back. The picture was of a single sheep grazing in a green field, behind it the silhouette of an oak tree and a pale blue sky" (p. 158).

Read Matthew 9:36.

10. What are sheep without a shepherd like?

_____

Read John 10:14-18 and 27-19.

STUDY GUIDE

11. What does this tell you about the path of the Shepherd?

___

___

Read Ezekiel 34: 11-15.

12. How does God feel about the lost sheep? What does he want to do for them?

___

___

___

When our son was young, I studied the "rod" of the shepherd in Proverbs to try to get a handle on what the rod of correction meant when it came to disciplining our children. What I discovered was that the staff of the Shepherd was used to lovingly and gently guide the sheep. When one of them started to wander, the shepherd would tap the sheep on its side to keep it in the fold so it wouldn't get separated from the pack and eaten by wolves. When a sheep was very stubborn and wouldn't listen to the shepherd, only then would he have to give that sheep a strong whack to teach it to stay in the fold where it would be safe.

> **Highlighted Reading:** "When [God] says, 'Come over to this path—that one is hurting you or will hurt you' (for reasons we may not even comprehend)—do we *resist* the voice of the shepherd? Or do we come" (p. 159)?

Obeying the voice of the Shepherd is the key to finding the abundant life of the narrow road. One of the main things that prevented the Israelites from entering the promised land was that they returned to their former slavery via idolatry and disobedience. They wanted God's blessing, but they weren't willing to respect him as the all-knowing and all-loving Shepherd of their souls.

13. The Bible teaches that God disciplines those he loves. When you sense God correcting you, do you obey his guidance? Why or why not?

> **Highlighted Reading:** "Then I heard a voice...'Throw it out,' it said. 'Throw what out?' I asked aloud. 'The hash,' was the response...I looked down at the hash...I wanted *life* and I wanted *fruit* more than I wanted to live in this death any longer. And somehow I knew I had to choose. I picked up the cigarettes and the hash and walked to the bathroom. Shaking, I opened the satchel and let the broken brown clumps splatter into the toilet" (pp. 158-159).

This was not the last time I threw out my idols. In fact, I wandered in the desert for a while, going back and forth between following the Shepherd's voice and resisting it.

The Path of Obedience

Read Romans 6:11-23.

14. What do these verses say to you?

Sin always sounds good at the time; otherwise people wouldn't do it. When we follow the narrow path, we show that we love God more than we love our sin. As Psalm 66:18-19 says, "If I had cherished sin in my heart, the Lord would not have listened, but

STUDY GUIDE

God has surely listened and heard my voice in prayer."

We have to get real with ourselves. Where our treasure is, there our heart will be also." As long as we cherish sin in our hearts, we will be slaves to it. As long as we cherish Christ in our hearts, we will be slaves to righteousness. To be a slave to God is to be free. That's God's economy for you! Upside down, upside down!

15. Write Romans 6:22 here:

16. What is the benefit to being a slave to righteousness?

Soon we are going to cross the Jordan. Before we do, I implore you to answer the next two questions:

17. Is there any sin in your life that you know deep down you need to repent of? What is it?

18. Are there any idols you need to throw out like "menstrual cloths" and say "Away with you!"? (Isa. 30:22) Do that here:

There's no other way I can say it than this: Obedience brings blessing. Try it! As Shane always says, "Test it." Try doing things God's way for one year, he says, and see what happens. You always have the option of going back to your old life. Remember, in the garden, we were free to choose. You can choose to obey him or not.

But I believe the Perfect Path is the path of obedience. Why? Because it leads to the pasture; it leads to rest.

The Path of Rest

Finally, the Perfect Path is the path of rest. As our verse of the day says, "Ask for the ancient paths, ask where the good way is, and walk in it, and you will find rest for your souls" (Jeremiah 6:16). Obeying the voice of the Shepherd brings rest.

Read Matthew 11:28-30.

19. What does this tell you about the path of following Christ?

_____

_____

_____

Read John 10:9-10.

20. For those of us who enter through the narrow gate, what will we find there?

    Circle one:

    Wandering   Pain   Pasture

21. What do you think pasture represents?

_____

22. Fill in the blank:

    "The thief comes only to steal and kill and destroy; I have come that they may have _____."

Read Psalms 107:4-9.

Some of us have wandered in desert wastelands, finding no way to a place where we could settle. We have called out for direction and cried out for peace. God offers to lead us along a "straight way" where he will satisfy us and fill us with good things.

This leads us to our eighth truth. Our eighth lie was, "The wide road has much more to offer and leads to satisfaction." Our eighth truth crushes that lie: "The narrow road has much more to offer and leads to the satisfaction of your soul."

Truth #8
The narrow road has much more to offer and leads to the satisfaction of your soul.

Even when we don't know exactly where we are going, as long as we follow him, we are on the Perfect Path. His Presence is with us; we are being shepherded by the all-wise and loving Shepherd; and his path is not one that is burdensome and laden with things that weigh us down. Instead, his path leads where our souls desire to go, the land of satisfaction.

How might God want you to respond to what he's revealed to you today?

_____

_____

_____

To be satisfied, to be fulfilled: this is the quest of every human, and the topic of our next chapter. Thank you for taking this journey with me, for trusting God's leading through tumultuous waters. As promised, we will find fruitful vineyards on the other side.

Girl Perfect Readings

Chapter 9—The Perfect Fulfillment:
The Road to Healing

Chapter 10—The Perfect Freedom:
A Beautiful Mosaic

Lessons

26: Our Food

27: Healing Waters

28: Freedom to be the Girl God Made

29: Free Indeed

30: Canaan

Lesson 26
Our Food

Read or reread *Girl Perfect*, Chapter 9, "The Perfect Fulfillment."
Verse of the Day: "My cup runneth over..." Psalms 23:5 (KJV)

Lie #9
You can fulfill and heal yourself.

The Longing:
Fulfillment and Healing

In the Wilderness

After the Israelites crossed the Red Sea, they traveled without water for three days and became very thirsty. They complained to Moses, and he cried out to God, who then supplied them with sweet water to drink.

Read Exodus 15:24-27.

1. Fill in the blank:

    After he gave them the water, God tells them to pay close attention to his commands, for "I am the Lord, who _____ you." (15:26)

2. After that, how many springs of water did he lead them to?

    _____

3. Where did they camp?

Then, the Israelites got hungry and bitterly complained that they had more food in slavery than they did in the wilderness. Once again, God heard their need and provided them with food.

Read Exodus 16:2-4 and 11-18.

4. What did they accuse Moses of bringing them into the desert to do? (16:3)

5. Write here what the Lord said to Moses in verse 4 (the first sentence):

6. According to verse 18, did the people have:

    Circle one:
    Not enough to satisfy their hunger
    Too much and lots of the bread went to waste
    As much as they needed

Read Exodus 16:31-35.

7. Why do you think they were told to preserve the manna for generations to come?

8. Did God satisfy their needs all the way to the border of Canaan?

I Am the Bread

> **Highlighted Reading:** "I am living off the brown, tattered pages of this little Good News Bible, my soul absorbing each word like bits of Communion bread" (p. 174).

Read Deuteronomy 8:1-3.

9. According to this passage, on what does man live?

> **Highlighted Reading:** "I can get stuck in the forest at night; I can find a way back. But I cannot, I will not, go on without the Word…With…a desperate spirit, I sprint back along the shore of the river…Then I run another mile or so back to the bank...then I step on it. I step on that tender book, lying quietly at the side of the rushing water, waiting for me. I tuck it into my chest…I have my food" (p. 175).

Read John 6:32-35 and 47-58.

10. Who is the "true bread from heaven"?

11. What is Jesus saying about the difference between manna and himself?

12. If the bread is his body, what do you think his blood symbolizes?

   _____

I Am the Water

> **Highlighted Reading:** "...A sixteen-year-old girl named Naomi comes bounding in from the back of the church exclaiming: 'Jenny-fair! I have found you an English Bible! You can read it! It is the Good News!' ... When she hands it to me, it is as if she hands me a glass of cool water. It is that simple. There is no deep, theological discussion, no mindful study, no political debate. It is a glass of water being handed to a very, very thirsty girl, and I take it. (p. 156).

Read John 4:10-13.

13. What is Jesus saying he is? What do you think it means to "never thirst"?

   _____

   _____

   _____

14. Evaluate your relationship with the Word. Is it bread and water to you? Or do you only come to it when you are desperate? Use the space here to share what the Word means to you and what this lesson has taught you it should mean to you:

   _____

   _____

   _____

After all his hard work leading the people through the desert, Moses never got to enter the promised land. Just before the Israelites crossed the Jordan River, Moses passed the torch to Joshua. Shortly before Moses died, he said of God's Commandments, "They are not just idle words for you; they are your life" (Deut. 32:47).

To Be Full

> **Highlighted Reading:** "We are born with longings. We long for love, peace, happiness, hope, and a future. We long to be known, seen, loved, and above all, we long to be healed and fulfilled. These longings become caverns within us if they are not satisfied" (p. 176).

In the words of Psalm 42:1, "As the deer pants for streams of water, so my soul pants for you, O God." This entire study has been about how we human beings fill our God-given longings. While we are on this earth, Satan will keep on lying to us. "You can fulfill and heal yourself," he lies, attempting to stab God right in the heart. The prince the world promises we can find satisfaction apart from our Maker; and almost worse, that we can heal ourselves; we can "pick ourselves up by the bootstraps" and get well on our own, without the Great Physician's help.

I wonder how that makes God feel—maybe like this:

> *I made you and I know you. I have what you need—water from the Rock; manna raining down, settling like my compassion, the morning dew. I offer food that will satisfy and love that won't run out. Why do you turn to the lies and feed on ashes when I can make your hearts swell and throb with life?*

Read Isaiah 55:1-2.

15. What do you think is "the richest of fare"? What is God saying to us here?

_____

_____

Finally, read Psalm 23.

After all we have studied, how do these verses hold new meaning for you? I have written them here for your study. After each verse, share what it means to you:

The Lord is my shepherd, I shall not be in want.

He makes me lie down in green pastures,

he leads me beside quiet waters, he restores my soul.

He guides me in paths of righteousness for his name's sake.

Even though I walk through the valley of the shadow of death,

I will fear no evil, for you are with me;

your rod and your staff, they comfort me.

You prepare a table before me in the presence of my enemies.

You anoint my head with oil; my cup overflows.

Surely goodness and love will follow me all the days of my life,

and I will dwell in the house of the Lord forever.

In this crazy world, we are all looking for that which would just *fill* us. God promises he can fill our cups until they "overflow," until "streams of living water" flow from within.

Let's close this day with a picture of our souls when we are with God one day:

"Never again will they hunger; never again will they thirst. The sun will not beat upon them, nor any scorching heat. For the Lamb at the center of the throne will be their shepherd; he will lead them to springs of living water. And God will wipe away every tear from their eyes" (Revelation 7:16-17).

> How might God want you to respond to what he's revealed to you today?

Lesson 27
Healing Waters

Verse of the Day: "…For I am the Lord, who heals you." Exodus 15:26

Not only can his living water fill us, but it can also flush out all things former and be the healing water that rushes through the longings of our hearts, cleansing them through and through.

Crossing the Jordan

At the very beginning of this study, I gave you a pep talk taken from the one God gave Joshua before he led the people across the Jordan. Now you are going to read it for yourself from the Scriptures.

Read Joshua 1:1-9.

1. What do these words mean to you?

_____

_____

_____

Read Joshua 3:1-4.

The leaders told the people to follow the ark of the covenant and those who were carrying it so the people would know which way to go because they had never been that way before. The ark of the covenant held the sacred treasures of God's people in a gold box with two cherubim (angels) facing each other on the lid. Inside, the ark held the stone tablets of the Ten Commandments, a jar of manna, and Aaron's staff, which represented authority. Covenant means "promise." We might look at it this way: as they were about to go a way they had not gone before, they had to carry with them all they had learned from their slavery, deliverance, and wandering in the wilderness. In the ark of the covenant, they carried sacred items that revealed sacred truths: 1) God's commands would be their very life; 2) the Lord would provide all they needed; and 3) they could trust the leadership of Aaron — they could follow a free man to freedom, if you know what I mean.

But the final authority in leading his people was God's and God's alone. Carrying these truths with them, they stepped into the edge of the Jordan River, knowing that only God could make a straight path; only he could part the sea.

Read Joshua 3:14-17.

Following God can be scary at times, not because we can't trust him, but because we don't usually know quite where we are going. As the water of the Jordan River rushed back in a mighty tide, it made high, steep walls on either side of the pathway so that an entire nation could travel through. I am sure the people could not hear the voices of their leaders over the thunderous sound of the river being divided asunder by God's mighty hand. They could not see God's face or even his back, but they knew his power reigned.

To follow him is to lay hold of the promise: a land flowing with milk and honey is waiting on the other side.

Healing

> **Highlighted Reading:** "On day three, I take a train to the next town and find it desolate. While sitting on a bridge, feet dangling over the water, I hear bells tolling in the distance. Then a boy races by me in long strides, with a book in his hand. Curious, I follow him to a church square where the townspeople have gathered. I file in with them

> and sit down, not comprehending a word of the sermon except 'Jesus,' yet I weep the entire time, tears streaming down my face as I bow my head so that no one can see me...'Heal me,' I whisper. 'Please heal me'" (pp. 173-174).

As God begins to fulfill us, a simultaneous phenomenon occurs: his living water rushes into the cracks, crevasses, and gorges of our little-girl hearts, cleansing them through and through. As he fills us, he heals us.

I was very ill when I cried that day in that nameless church in that nameless city (I don't even know what the town was called.) I remember there were two girls sitting on either side of me, obviously noticing I was crying. I hid my face behind the veil of my hair and wept; that little girl inside of me, so far from home and so alone, could only cry privately from the loss of it all.

2. I know what it is to hurt. I don't know what hurts in you, though. But you do. Please use this space to share what hurts:

_____

_____

_____

_____

_____

_____

_____

_____

Emotional Healing

> **Highlighted Reading:** "Deep wounds, however, take time to heal. Medically speaking, some wounds cannot just be medicated and sewn closed. Sometimes raw wounds need to remain wide open for a long time, cleaned, and treated over and over until finally they are safe to be closed. They must heal from the inside out" (p. 190).

3. Are you willing to keep your heart wide open to God, so that he can wash his living water through it? Share here how you plan to do that:

_____

_____

_____

_____

> **Highlighted Reading:** "As I began to open my heart... free, unconditional love was able to reach those empty places that I had long ago sewn closed...Over time, it smoothed out the most jagged pieces that once broke off my heart" (p. 191).

Healing is a tough thing to put words to; it's something that happens from the inside out instead of the outside in. Masks block healing. Satan's masquerade is the act of trying to create beauty from the outside in.

But Jesus works from the inside out.

Read Luke 9:28-32.

4. What did the disciples see here? Circle one:

   His robe
   His possessions
   His glory

Yes, they saw Jesus's glory. As he miraculously transfigured before their eyes, his beauty on the inside came radiating out.

Read 2 Corinthians 4:16-18.

The more we come to him, face-to-face and unveiled, the more he transfigures us, healing us from the inside out. And with unveiled faces, we begin to reflect the Lord's glory, with ever-increasing glory.

Please turn now back to the beginning of our journey, the beginning to this book, and review what you wrote there about your little-girl heart, masks, and perfection.

5. How have you grown during this journey?

   _____
   _____
   _____
   _____
   _____

6. What have you learned about the masquerade?

   _____
   _____
   _____
   _____

7. What have you learned about your little-girl heart? What does she need? What does she long for? How can she get those longings filled?

The ninth lie was: "You can fulfill and heal yourself." It isn't true, is it? In fact, it's the furthest thing from the truth. I know because I lived the lie, and now I'm living the truth. It's not all perfect, but it's being healed. In the writing of this study, the deepest lesions of my heart have been exposed and are in various stages of healing. I don't know what this study has meant for you. But for me, it's been like a baptism, like a rebirth. I feel closer to my little-girl heart than ever.

Has anything within you been healed during this journey? If so, take the time to share it here. There will be a day when you will look back on this and marvel at how much he has healed in you.

As we allow him to fulfill us, his living water will go to the very places within that we think no light can reach. There, in the depths of our little-girl hearts, as long as we stay open to him, he will fulfill our greatest longing of all: to be healed. Our ninth truth is: "When we allow God to fulfill us, he will also heal us."

Truth #9
When we allow God to fulfill us,
he will also heal us.

And, as we know, the ultimate healing will come at the final unveiling, when we get to see him face- to-face, glory-to-glory.

> How might God want you to respond to what he's revealed to you today?
>
> _____
>
> _____
>
> _____

Lesson 28
Freedom to be the Girl God Made

Read or reread *Girl Perfect*, Chapter 10, "The Perfect Freedom." Verse of the Day: "When perfection comes, the imperfect disappears." 1 Corinthians 13:10

Lie #10
Freedom is the ability to go wherever you want with no one controlling you.

The Longing:
Freedom

The Longing to Be Free

The world has an interesting view of freedom. It's basically: do what you want, when you want, for whatever reason you want. Could you hear all the "yous" in that last sentence? The world's view of freedom is self-gratification.

Once again, God's economy is the reverse: "Delight yourself in the Lord and he will give you the desires of your heart" (Ps. 37:4).

1. What does this verse mean to you?

_____
_____
_____

Our little-girl hearts long for so much. They long for affirmation and acceptance; they long to be received without judgment; they long to be beautiful; they long to be applauded; they long for joy, peace, direction, fulfillment, and healing.

Read Proverbs 13:12.

2. Write it here:

_____

_____

_____

3. After this journey through the longings of our little-girl hearts, what does this verse mean to you?

_____

_____

Listening to lies makes our hearts sick. They always sound good at first, but they leave us ill within, longing all the more. But "a longing fulfilled is sweet to the soul" (Prov. 13:19).

I'd venture to say the swim has been worth it. I know it has for me. It's been worth it because we have found that which will quench our soul hunger; we have found what is the "sweet nectar of childhood," the simplicity of getting our longings filled right in our own backyards.

Follow Your Heart

> **Highlighted Reading:** "Now, each morning, I inhale the dense, sweet scent of flowers wafting through the air. Carefully, I place the best arrangements on the sidewalk and hang the trailing roses. The shop is quaint and has a very slow but steady stream of customers. I earn minimum

> wage selling someone else's flowers, but I don't worry about how I look…In the complicated world of fashion and photography, I discovered that all I ever wanted was a simple life" (p. 188).

If there was one thing I could leave you with as we approach the last days of our journey together, it would be this: Follow your heart.

4. What would it look like for you to follow your heart?

_____

5. What are the most important things to you? What really matters?

_____

Freedom to Be You

> **Highlighted Reading:** Faith gives us the freedom to be the girls God made—freedom to be a mess…freedom to be real; freedom to follow our hearts. Faith gave me freedom… to fly, despite the low places I had been. It gave me dignity, worth, value. It made me stand tall. It me to go home, imperfect. If freed me from my sin, and it freed me to be me" (pp. 188-189).

6. What has faith done for you?

   _____

   _____

   _____

7. If you were "free to be you," what would you be free to be?

   _____

   _____

   _____

Freedom from Perfect

Delivering this study guide has broken one last iron chain around my heart. I've had to let go, completely – let go of control; let go of my ability to do anything without holding on for dear life to that Righteous Branch who roots me and gives me strength. And the truth is, it's still not perfect enough for my stupid desire to get it perfect!

So, I hereby give up the ability to communicate how Beautiful and Glorious Christ is; I give up. I take these humble baskets of bread I have presented you in this study and ask that God turn them into more than enough to feed your soul; and I pray that he turns them into loaves to feed thousands.

> **Highlighted Reading:** "Letting go of perfect is letting go of the temporary. It is fixing our eyes on the eternal. It is getting our eyes off the demands of the world and fixing them on God…It is experiencing the real freedom Christ died for—freedom to be able to shrug off the imperfections, to laugh, to cultivate joy…" (p. 194).

8. What does "freedom from perfect" look like for you?

Read 1 Corinthians 13:10.

9. Write 1 Corinthians 13:10 here:

> **Highlighted Reading:** "Perfect will come back for us one day and take us home, forever" (p. 194).

10. What will happen when Perfection comes?

Hebrews 2:10 says that Jesus was made perfect through his suffering on the cross, and Hebrews 10:14 says that by that one sacrifice, he has made "perfect forever" those who are being made holy. That's us, my friend. As we gaze into the "perfect law that gives freedom," we become more and more like him; we become holy. He didn't say he would make us imperfect; he said he would make us perfect. And that's what we've been in search of all along.

Before I left Munich, I took out that old canvas with the wicked, painted scene of hell on it and drew a beautiful cross with Jesus on it, rising. He became my "Perfect."

11. How is he your "Perfect"? How does knowing Christ wash away all the imperfections?

    How might God want you to respond to what he's revealed to you today?

Close your time today in prayer. Only two days together left! I can hardly believe it.

Lesson 29
Free Indeed

Verse of the Day: "So if the Son sets you free, you will be free indeed." John 8:36

Speaking the Truth of Your Life

> **Highlighted Reading:** "Over time, he has also freed me to speak the truth of my life without fearing what people think" (p.189).

Reread this verse that I used to open the book, *Girl Perfect*:

> *Then, leaving her water jar, the woman went back to the town and said to the people, "Come, see a man who told me everything I ever did. Could this be the Christ"?... Many of the Samaritans from that town believed in him because of the woman's testimony. (John 4:28-29, 39)*

The woman at the well had tried a lot of things to fill her "water jar," that place of longing inside of her soul. She had believed the world's lies, and they had left her deluded and cast aside. Then there came One who promised her living water that could fill all of her empty places.

That water is the Spirit.

Read our verse, 2 Corinthians 3:16-18, again.

1. Write verse 17 here:

   _____

   _____

So many of us don't share our testimonies because we are afraid of what people might think if we actually spoke the truth of our lives. But I spoke the truth of my life in *Girl Perfect*, and it has impacted you in some way; if it hadn't, you wouldn't have gotten this far in the journey; you would have given up. (And I am so proud of you for not giving up!) I believe so strongly in taking off the masks, getting real, and speaking truth. Why? Because "where the Spirit of the Lord is, there is freedom…" There is freedom from accusation and freedom from condemnation. We are literally freed up to use our lives for good. There is nothing more freeing than honesty, and nothing can hold us back more than masks.

Your Mosaic

> **Highlighted Reading:** "I once had a dream that I was standing on a stage, speaking to an audience. On the table before me were porcelain masks from my childhood collection, and there was a hammer in my hand. I began smashing the masks with the hammer. As the blows fell down on their perfect faces, they exploded and shards sprayed all over the stage. In the dream I was happy." (p. 192).

2. Smash your masks. List here the masks you have worn and smash them. Cross them out; color over them; do whatever feels right to express how they no longer control you.

_____

_____

> **Highlighted Reading:** "And my Creator has lovingly, patiently, picked up every broken shard and placed them back together in a mosaic that is more beautiful than they ever were whole" (p. 192).

3. If God took every broken piece of your little-girl heart and put it back together as a way to shine a light of hope for others, what would that look like? How does or could God use your past to point others to himself?

___

The Real Battle

The voice that tells us we can't speak the truth of our lives through our testimonies is the voice of the accuser.

Read Ephesians 6:10-18.

When the Israelites crossed the Jordan into the land of Canaan, it wasn't all perfect. Here were giants to face and great battles to be waged for them to conquer the land. They had to hold on tight to their faith that God would destroy their enemies and gain the victory so they could enjoy the land of promise. The same goes for our Canaan, our return to our little-girl hearts. Everything on earth will battle for the territory of our hearts. And it is a spiritual battle.

4. According to Ephesians 6:12, what is our struggle against?

___

Read Colossians 2:15.

5. How did Jesus disarm the "powers and authorities"?

_____

_____

Read Revelation 12:9-11.

6. With what two things do we overcome Satan?

_____

_____

Our tenth lie was, "Freedom is the ability to go wherever you want with no one controlling you." That's a laughable one. No, mr. deceiver, no. When the devil tempted Jesus in the wilderness, Jesus looked him square in the eye and spoke truth to him. When the apostles were confronted with evil, they looked directly at it and spoke truth. Our tenth truth shatters that lie: Only Christ can set us free. By the blood of the Lamb, we are free indeed.

Truth #10
Only Christ can set us free.

Second, we overcome the evil one with our testimonies. My friend, I encourage you to share your testimony. There is power in your testimony—in your story. We all have a story. We all have lessons we have learned and beauty within; we all have had triumphs and trials. Just remember these words: "Many…believed in him *because of the woman's testimony.*"

No study that deals with real beauty in God's eyes would be complete without this last verse:

Read Isaiah 52:7.

7. Write it here:

   How might God want you to respond to what he's revealed to you today?

Close your time in prayer.

Lesson 30
My Canaan

Verse of the Day: "If anyone hears my voice and opens the door, I will come in and eat with him, and he with me." Revelation 3:20

Well, it's been a wild swim. Thank you for traveling so far and so wide with me. Thank you for tackling the tough stuff, for getting real, and opening your heart. My hope and prayer for you is that you keep that little-girl heart wide open. It's a tough world, I know. But we are called to be strong. We are "more than conquerors" (Rom. 8:37). Like Dorothy in *The Wizard of Oz*, we have discovered that the longings of our hearts can be filled right where we are, in our own backyards. Here, in our personal lands of Canaan, abundance is fully possible.

The abundant life has nothing to do with perfection. Here on earth, things will always be kind of messy. But we serve a perfect God. And he wants the best for us, always. On the last page, I have given you a list of the truths, the lies, and the longings we have studied. Don't forget the lies and how they cheat us out of getting those God-given longings filled; and embed those truths into your heart.

And be real. That is the best advice I can give you.

The following is a picture of my Canaan. After that comes a page for you to write yours.

> *Our family lives in North Texas now. It's not supposed to snow here. But the other day, when I was writing about Munich, it snowed all day. Miniature tufts of white cotton, falling in a swift, steady descent. I was sitting at my new kitchen table, looking out the window, remembering how in Munich I longed for someone to come and eat with me. I used to set the table for two then, wishing someone could love me at my worst.*

"Here I am! I stand at the door and knock," you said to me, Lord, "If anyone hears my voice and opens the door, I will come in and eat with him, and he with me" (Rev. 3:20). My Jesus has been eating with me ever since.

I made spaghetti for fifty people the other day. I know many of the women who came to my home wondered why I didn't just make it easy and order out. But as I stood over the cauldrons of sauce, slowly stirring them the way the signora had taught me, I just shrugged my shoulders and smiled. Little did they know all the concrete jungles I traversed to get to the signora's garden. She reminded me of my little-girl heart, of what truly matters: family. She taught me to look people in the eyes and to go home.

As I wipe my bread along the rim of my bowl, soaking up the leftover sauce, I am so grateful for this new table where I sit. Today the tabletop is scattered with three worn-out Bibles, the delicate, falling-out pages covered with highlights and sticky notes; four journals are stacked in an array, the yellow one open to the middle. Its spine when laid on its back makes the pages fan open wide. Later, around this table my family will gather.

Our daughter Olivia will set out plates, cups, and forks; Zach will eat every last bite; and Sam and Daddy will clear when we are finished. Usually, I cook and Shane makes the kids do the dishes. Mostly, he makes us laugh, chases, jumps out of corners, plays. He is the laughter.

I know it's all a gift; humanity, health, and life on earth are precarious things; we never know how long they'll last.

But when you wandered like I did for so long, you don't ever want to go back; you want to stay in the pasture. When we are wounded, he will carry us; when we need protection, he will give it. These things I know.

Tears gather on my cheeks. I'm writing again, and when I'm writing, I am so happy. These days I speak in churches, schools, wherever. And I keep telling the same story, again and again. I don't want to ever tire of telling it. By the blood of the Lamb and the word of our testimony, we shall overcome.

"Even when I am old and gray, do not forsake me, God, till I declare your power to the next generation, your might to all who are to come." Psalm 71:18

The next page is for you.

With all my heart,

Jen

Your Canaan

A Worksheet: What Is Perfect?

Take the space below to say in a few sentences what you learned about each "perfect".

The Perfect Affirmation

The Perfect Acceptance

The Perfect Image

The Perfect Body

The Perfect Look

The Perfect Dream

The Perfect Escape

The Perfect Path

The Perfect Fulfillment

The Perfect Freedom

The Lies, The Longings, and The Truths That Set Us Free

Lie #1:	Your affirmation comes from men.
The Longing:	Affirmation
The Twist:	To receive affirmation from boys and men, you must be sexy and sexual.
Truth #1:	Perfect affirmation comes from God alone.

Lie #2:	Looking at other women/girls shows how you measure up.
The Longing:	Acceptance
Truth #2:	Christ says, "I give you a perfect acceptance. Now you give it to others."

Lie #3:	If something looks good on the outside, it is good on the inside.
The Longing:	To Be Received
Truth #3:	God says, "Man sees the outside, but I see the heart."

Lie #4:	If you can control your body, you are in control of your life.
The Longing:	To Be Beautiful
The Twist:	Your body must be perfect to receive the praise of the world.
Truth #4:	God says, "Your body on earth will never be perfect, but as I fill it with my perfect beauty, you can release control to me."

Lie #5:	If you've got it, flaunt it!

The Longing:	To Be Applauded
Truth #5:	God says, "You were created to reflect my beauty, not yours. Pride in external beauty is from the devil himself. The most beautiful look you can ever have is the heart of my Son."

Lie #6:	If you are successful and rich, you will be happy.
The Longing:	Joy
Truth #6:	God says, "Money and position will never fully satisfy you; you were created for relationship with me, and only discovering my dream for your life will bring you joy."

Lie #7:	If you are in pain, the things of the world will bring you peace.
The Longing:	Peace
Truth #7:	Only Jesus brings peace.

Lie #8:	The wide road has much more to offer and leads to satisfaction.
The Longing:	Direction
Truth #8:	The narrow road has much more to offer and leads to the satisfaction of your soul.

Lie #9:	You can fulfill and heal yourself.
The Longing:	Fulfillment and Healing
Truth #9:	When we allow God to fulfill us, he will also heal us.

Lie #10:	Freedom is the ability to go wherever you want with no one controlling you.
The Longing:	Freedom
Truth #10:	Only Christ can set us free.

Notes

Lessons 1-5
1. All Definitions Taken From Merriam-Webster's Online Dictionary: http://www.merriam-webster.com/.
2. Beth Moore, Breaking Free: Making Liberty In Christ A Reality In Life Workbook Edition (Nashville: Lifeway Press, 1999), 101.

Lessons 11-15
1. "Get The Facts: Body Image," https://now.org/now-foundation/love-your-body/love-your-body-whats-it-all-about/get-the-facts/.
2. Campaign For Real Beauty, "Body Talk: Building Body Confidence," http://www.campaignforrealbeauty.com/dsef/pdfs/bodytalk_excerpt.pdf.
3. "Get The Facts: Body Image," ibid.
4. Dr. Lake Linardon, "Body Image Statistics 2023: 52+ Shocking Facts & Stats, March 3, 2023, accessed May 2, 2023, https://breakbingeeating.com/body-image-statistics/#Body_Image_Statistics_for_Women
5. Dr. Lake Linardon, ibid.
6. "Get The Facts: Body Image," ibid.
7. Campaign For Real Beauty, ibid.
8. Dr. Lake Linardon, ibid.
9. Dr. Lake Linardon, ibid.
10. Dr. Lake Linardon, ibid.
11. Sari Fine Shepphird, Ph.D., "Our 'Size Zero' Culture," Encyclopedia Brittanica Blog, February 3, 2009, http://www.britannica.com/blogs/2009/02/the-size-zero-debate-alive-and-well/.
12. Johann Hari, "Why Have We Stopped Raging Against The Sick, Sick Fashion Industry"?, The Huffington Post, September 15, 2009, http://www.huffingtonpost.com/johann-hari/why-have-we-stopped-ragin_b_287915.html.
13. Gurian, "How To Raise Girls With Healthy Self-Esteem."
14. Jo Couzens, "Almost 50% Of 11-16 Year-Old Girls

Dieting," Sky News Online, November 3, 2009, http://news.sky.com/skynews/home/uk-news/young-girls-unhappy-with-appearance-consider-cosmetic-surgery-and-diets/article/200911115430845.
15. Sari Fine Shepphird, Ph.D.,"More Kids Today Are Unhappy With Their Bodies," Eating Disorders Blogs, August 29, 2009, http://www.eatingdisordersblogs.com/treatment_notes/2009/08/more-kids-today-are-unhappy-with-their-bodies.html.
16. Jack London, Martin Eden (New York: Penguin Books, 1984), 17.

Lessons 16-20
1. For More Information On Ezekiel 28, Visit www.whatthebibleteaches.com/wbt_510.htm, www.piney.com/theod.ezek.28.html, and www.jfb.biblecommenter.com/ezekiel/28.htm.
2. "Dating Abuse Statistics," http://www.chooserespect.org/scripts/teens/statistics.asp.
3. "Domestic Violence Stats," http://www.dvrc-or.org/domestic/violence/resources/c61/.
4. "I Said A Prayer For You Today" Credited To Frank J. Zamboni In Favorite Catholic Prayers (Ny: Regina Press Malhame & Company, 1996).
5. Into The Wild, Written And Directed By Sean Penn (Hollywood, Ca: Paramount Vantage And River Road Entertainment, 2007).

Lessons 21-25
1. Bob Murray, Ph.D. And Alicia Fortinberry, M.S., "Depression Facts And Stats," http://www.upliftprogram.com/depression_stats.html.
2. Webmd, "Depression In Women," 2010, http://www.webmd.com/depression/guide/depression-women.
3. Laurel Slade, M.S., "The Triangle Of Depression," Worksheet.
4. Ibid.
5. Murray And Fortinberry.
6. Barent W. Walsh, Ph.D., Treating Self-Injury (Ny: The Guilford Press, 2008).

7. Janette Davenport, M.S., L.P.C., "The Truth About Cutting And Self-Harm," http://www.sunrisertc.com/articles/truth-about-cutting-and-self-harm.php

If You're a Fan of this Study Guide, Please Tell Others...

- Write about *Girl Perfect* and the *Girl Perfect Study Guide* on your social media page and tag **@jenniferstrickland_author**.

- Write a positive review of *Girl Perfect* and the *Girl Perfect Study Guide* on www.amazon.com

- Suggest the book and study guide to friends.

- Lead a book club or study group through *Girl Perfect*.

- Send Jennifer suggestions on websites, conferences, ministries, and events you know of where this study guide could be offered.

- Reach out to Jennifer and share how this study impacted your life. She'd love to hear from you!

- Purchase additional copies to give away as gifts.

Connect With Me...

- Please go to **www.girlperfectbook.com** to get everything you need to lead a group through the *Girl Perfect Study Guide*.

- To learn more about Jennifer Strickland Ministries, please visit **www.jenniferstrickland.net**.

- Find Jen on social media at **@jenniferstrickland_author**.

Relevant, honest, and insightful, Jennifer's books, studies, and videos embrace the beauty and adversity of being a woman in this world. With heartfelt compassion and insight into today's young people, Jennifer offers individual and group study through her non-profit ministry, www.URMore.org.

Made in United States
North Haven, CT
17 June 2024